Cat, thy NAME is Edith

Cat, thy NAME is EDITH

by Roz Young

Orange Frazer Press

Wilmington, Ohio

ILLUSTRATIONS by LINDA SCHARF

"The Cat and the Moon" as reprinted with permission of Macmillan Publishing Company from The Poems of W. B. Yeats: A New Edition edited by Richard J. Finneran. Copyright 1919 by Macmillan Publishing Company. Renewed 1947 by Bertha Georgie Yeats.

"The Best Bed" as reprinted from The Cats Cradle Book by Sylvia Townsend Warner, with permission of the publishers, Chatto and Windus, Random Century Group Limited, 20 Vauxhall Bridge Road, London SW1V 2SA.

Library of Congress Catalog Card Number: 91-062479

ISBN 0-9619637-7-8

Published by Orange Frazer Press, Inc.
Main Street, Box 214
Wilmington, Ohio 45177

For Tinker Bell

benevolent despot of the William and Peggy Self family

FOREWORD

Edith is a cat of cats. She is patient, gracious, loyal, agile, beautiful, and inscrutable. She never saw a rubber band she didn't try to swallow, and when she is around no flower is safe in its vase.

She has been kidnapped, marooned, and lost. She is the only cat in Dayton, Ohio with her own file at the newspaper office, and her own hymnal in church. (She is Episcopalian). She is the only cat in Dayton history to be the VIP honoree riding on the back of a convertible in a parade right up the middle of Main Street.

Many of Edith's escapades have been regaling local readers of the *Dayton Daily News* since she was a kitten. Now the stories have been rewritten and others gathered and added into a book in time for her eighth birthday.

The author takes this opportunity to express appreciation to the publisher, the editor, her colleagues on the paper, and the readers for their kindly reception of Edith. As for Edith herself — well, you know how cats are.

Roz Young
Dayton, Ohio
July, 1991

Cat, thy NAME
is Edith

Enter Edna

Out of the cardboard box popped two pink-lined furry ears, a pair of chartreuse-gold eyes, a set of fawn-colored whiskers, and two brown-and-beige paws. A kitten jumped from the box, landing on the carpet with never a sound.

She looked at my friend Catharine and then at me.

"Ow," she said, opening a mouth about the size of a dime.

"Now what happens?" I asked.

"Just let her look around. Cats explore whenever they go into a new place. Not to worry."

Not to worry? How could I not worry? What is more, I was scared. It was easy for Catharine, who had had cats off and on all her life to say not to worry while Edna, striped tail hoisted straight up, disappeared into the dining room. I had never had a cat or dog or any kind of pet in my whole long life, and I couldn't help worrying.

Ever since Catharine and her husband Lewis had taken Blackwell, a seven-month-old kitten, into their home a few weeks before, she had been trying to persuade me to adopt one, too.

"I don't want a cat," I told her. "I'm happy without one."

"But you live alone. Nobody should live alone. A cat would be company and somebody to talk to."

I had lived alone so long I was used to it. After all, if you don't die young, you are bound to get old. Families die off — parents, husband, cousins — and if you were an only child, as I was, pretty soon you're the last leaf on the family tree. There isn't any supermarket that sells children or grandchildren or readymade families, that I know of.

"If I want somebody to talk to, I talk to myself or my potted plants."

"But a potted plant is not warm and soft and doesn't purr or sit in your lap at night."

"I have seen too many old ladies who are dotty about their dogs or cats or goldfish. I never want to be one of them," I said. "Have I ever told you about Vivian Jones? And remember the pet cemetery?"

One morning about two minutes before the opening bell the principal of Stivers High School, where I was teaching, came into my room.

"I'd like you to go down to Miss Jones's room and take attendance," he said. "And stay there until the substitute comes."

Teachers in public schools who have no home room and the first period unassigned often have to fill in for teachers whose cars won't start or who become ill about five minutes before it's time to start for school. They aren't happy about it because it means giving up a lesson-planning period, but it goes with the job.

"Is she ill?"

"No. Her dog died."

Her dog died? For heaven's sake, a teacher doesn't stay home from school because a dog died.

That shows how much I knew then about people and pets.

I had tried to have a kitten once. In the third grade or so I saw a kitten playing in a yard. Nobody was looking. I picked it up and carried it home.

My mother was getting lunch.

"Where did you get that kitty?"

"It followed me home." It was a lie and I expected to be struck down right there in the kitchen by God, who can see right through roofs, but nothing happened.

"Are you sure the kitten followed you? You didn't coax her?"

"I carried her a little. Will you let me keep her?"

She shook her head. "You know the rules. No kittens or puppies. Now you take that kitten right back where you found her."

"Before lunch?"

"Before lunch."

I took the kitten back and turned her loose in her own front yard. Lunch was ready when I got back.

I don't know why she wouldn't let me have a kitten or a puppy. I never asked her. I never asked her because one of her rules was there would never be any questioning of parental decisions. Another was that she would brook no arguments within the walls of our house.

"Brook no arguments" sounds rather quaint these days and almost Biblical. She always talked that way. She was a Sunday School teacher, a writer and a public speaker. When she spoke to my father and me, it was as if she were addressing the PTA or the Republican Club.

Another one of her edicts was there would be no whining on the part of the child in the house.

Every time the mother of John Prinz, the boy next door, asked him to run an errand or forbade him to do something he wanted to do, he whined. Whenever she heard him, Mother pointed out to me how horrible whining sounded. At those times I felt superior to John and every other child on our street because I never whined.

I thought about the kitten incident the morning I walked down to Vivian's room. To be truthful, I felt superior to people who carried on about their pets as if they were their babies. Vivian was one of those. She had bought Koko, a Basenji, when she read the book *Goodbye, My Lady.* She often talked about him as if he were a real person.

She was not one of the most popular members of the faculty. She was fat and often sarcastic, and you would have to search long and deep to find anything winsome about her at all. I would have felt less aggrieved about giving up a period for her if she had had a wreck on the way to school or was genuinely ill. Not a serious wreck, of course.

Not only did Vivian stay out of school that day, she stayed out for the next two days. The board of education's rule was that if a member of the immediate family died, the teacher could have three days off with pay. "Immediate family" meant parent, spouse or child. For a brother, sister or grandparent we could have one day off. Cousins did not count.

Several of us were lunching in the teacher's dining room the next payday when Vivian slammed her tray down so hard on the table, Nell Stafford dropped her fork.

"Sorry if I startled you," Vivian said, easing down

on her chair.

"Something bothering you?"

"If that man has a stroke some day," she said in a soft but deadly tone, "I hope I am the one who causes it."

No need to ask who "that man" was. Vivian often spoke of the principal in such a fashion.

"What did he do to you now?" I asked.

"He docked my pay because I stayed home when Koko died. It isn't fair. That dog meant more to me than any member of my family ever did." Her chin quivered as if she might cry.

"But you couldn't expect to get time off for that," Nell pointed out. "After all, he was just a dog."

Vivian banged down her fork and pushed back from the table.

"'Just a dog!' That is the unkindest remark anybody ever made to me. Nell Stafford, I never want to hear another word out of you as long as I live." With that she stalked out of the cafeteria.

Vivian and Nell still were not speaking several years later when I resigned from teaching to take a newspaper job on *The Journal Herald* in my home town of Dayton.

My job on the paper was to write a column three days a week about anything that struck me people would want to read. At times I also wrote feature stories for the Sunday magazine of the *Dayton Daily News*.

One day a photographer stopped at my desk.

"South of town between here and Lebanon," he said, "is The Pines Pet Cemetery. Have you ever been there?"

"No."

"Well, it's the damndest thing I ever saw. It's like a park. There are thousands of grave markers, monuments, statues, benches, and little red lanterns with candles burning in them. You have got to go down and take a look. I think it would make a story."

I drove down.

The Pines, owned by Jean Lawton, is a 35-acre grassy, rolling wooded area not far off the main highway. Since the cemetery opened in 1966, about eleven thousand animals have been buried there — goldfish, monkeys, birds, skunks, horses, dogs, and cats. The ashes of three human beings are buried there, too, surrounded by their pets.

The Pines is not unique. There are about five hundred pet cemeteries in the United States, most of them in the East and the Midwest. The first one was established at Hartsdale, N.Y., in 1896. A cat cemetery has been found at Luxor, Egypt, and a dog cemetery excavated at Peiping, China, has tombstones of marble, ivory, gold and silver.

A pet cemetery business provides the services of an undertaker as well as burial sites. The staff calls for a dead pet at the owner's home or veterinarian's office. In the office at The Pines is a display room where owners can choose a plastic casket, lined or unlined, a remembrance light, silk flowers, and a marker or monument. A remembrance light is a tube of red glass topped by a brass dome and cross. Owners may bring candles or purchase them at the office. The candles burn inside the cylinders for five hours and are lighted to memorialize pet birthdays or special days such as Christmas, Easter, and National Pet Memorial Day, the second Sunday in September.

On the grounds at The Pines is a small chapel for services or meditation. The chapel has four pews, candelabra, urns with greenery, and a guest register. Above the white wooden catalfaque hangs a bronze plaque that says, "If Christ had a little dog, he would have followed Him to the cross."

Jean Lawton says that about forty percent of the pet owners hold special burial services. Sometimes pet owners even bring their own clergyman.

While I walked around the cemetery looking at the graves, a white car drove slowly along the curving roadway and stopped. A white-haired woman stepped out of the car, walked to a small grave by the roadside, knelt down, and brushed away pine needles that had sifted over the grave and marker. She sat for a long time looking at the marker and running her hand over the letters. Then she rose, walked to the car, brought out a sheaf of tulip blossoms, and laid them on the grave.

She patted the ground, walked back to her car, and sat for a moment. Then she drove away.

The legend on the marker read: *Cricket, born 1958, died 1978*. Cricket had been at The Pines for twelve years.

I was amazed. What possessed a woman to visit a pet grave twelve years after the pet died? Why would anybody spend hundreds, even thousands, to bury a pet animal? And hold a real funeral with clergyman and all? I could understand children burying a pet in the backyard and putting flowers and perhaps a homemade cross on the grave. But grown-up men and women?

I drove back to the paper to write the story, still thinking downright strange the people who burned remembrance candles on pet's birthdays and spent fortunes on their grave monuments, and fussed over their animals as if they were their own children. Vivian, it seemed to me, was entirely out of line to stay out of school and expect the same consideration from the school board as if her mother or father died.

"You have told me the Vivian Jones story more than once," said Catharine, "and I read your feature story about the pet cemetery. You are wrong, wrong, wrong.

You have no idea what you have been missing. Somewhere there is a kitten that could make a huge difference in your life. Even if you don't believe me, I wish you would at least go with me to SICSA to look at them. I am thinking of getting a playmate for Blackwell."

SICSA — Society for the Improvement of the Condition of Stray Animals — is an adoption center for dogs and cats in our town. Animals needing homes are displayed in cages every weekend. Those nobody adopts are cared for in foster homes by volunteers until the next weekend. Volunteers also work raising funds and take kittens and puppies to nursing homes in the area.

"I will go with you," I said, "but that doesn't mean I will bring a cat home."

We went on a Saturday afternoon in January. SICSA is in an old frame house. Volunteers rush in and out, telephones ring, and people flock to look at the cats and dogs.

In row after row of wire cages in the basement kittens of all ages snoozed, played with toys, or gazed round-eyed at the visitors. We walked past cages holding white kittens, black kittens, orange ones, gray ones.

We came to a cage in which lay asleep with her nose on her paw a kitten with brown stripes and orange and fawn fur between the stripes. The card on the cage said her name was Edna, a brown-and-orange tabby, seven months old and very affectionate.

Catharine opened the cage door, picked Edna up and held her.

"Here," she said, "hold her for a minute."

I took her in my arms. She felt warm and soft and solid. She looked into my eyes with an unblinking green-gold gaze. She opened a wee mouth and said, "Ow."

When I looked into her eyes, something happened. Whatever it was almost made a click I could hear. I could no more put that warm, trusting kitten back into that cage than I could get into it myself.

Still I was cautious.

"Suppose I do take her home and it doesn't work out. Will you take her?"

"I promise," said Catharine.

I carried Edna to a desk at which sat a volunteer.

"Oh, are you going to adopt Edna?" she asked.

"It looks as if I am."

"That's wonderful. I know you'll love her. We have some papers here for you to sign."

Catharine held Edna while I read the papers. I had to promise to provide a good and adequate home for her, to accept financial responsibility for all vaccination and medical treatments, to have her spayed at a date recommended by her veterinarian, to keep a collar identification on her at all times, and not to transfer her to another home or animal shelter without notifying SICSA.

She had had several shots, and another was due in three weeks.

With shaking fingers I signed the papers. What was I doing?

In the SICSA office upstairs a volunteer told me I would need a carrying box, a litter pan, cat food, special dishes for food and water, and a toy or two.

Right away Edna objected to being put into the carrying box. She put an eye and then her nose to one of the holes. She stuck a wee paw through one. She cried.

As we left the building, my knees felt shaky. I had assumed the responsibility for the life of a furry person named Edna, and I was scared. What if she didn't like me? What if she became ill? What if she wouldn't eat? What if she ran away?

When Edna felt the motion of the car, she raised her voice in loud and pitiable cries. I tried to quiet her by poking my finger through the breathing hole and talking, but she would have none of it. She wanted out of that box and out of that car right now.

We carried Edna and all her paraphernalia into the house. Catharine set the litter box at the foot of the basement stairs and her food and water dishes in the kitchen by the cookbook shelves.

"How will she find the litter box?" I asked.

"All you have to do is show her once where it is," said Catharine. "Cats are very smart about litter boxes."

Edna toured the dining room, the bedroom, the office, the bathrooms, and the kitchen. Then she came back into the living room, sat down, and looked at us. We took her downstairs and showed her the litter box.

"I am going home now," said Catharine. "You will be all right."

It was quiet after Catharine left. I tiptoed around through the rooms looking for Edna, but she had vanished. I sat down and thought about what I had done. After a long time I heard a noise in the kitchen. Edna was eating out of her dish. She sat with her legs folded up under her and her tail straight out on the floor behind her.

I stood looking down at her. Edna wasn't a potted plant that would stay in one spot. She was fur and blood and bones and beautiful eyes, and she would walk around to places she wanted to go.

How would I manage with this new person in the house?

Exit Edna

The first thing to do was to think about her name.

Since mine is a literary household, I wanted her to have a literary name.

Somebody had already named her Edna. *The Oxford Dictionary of English Christian Names* says the etymology of *Edna* is unknown. The name does occur several places in Apocrypha, but that isn't much of a recommendation.

The first use of *Edna* in English literature is a character in *Hopes and Fears*, an 1860 novel by C.M. Yonge. That didn't recommend it, either. How many people ever heard of C.M. Yonge? As for *Hopes and Fears*, I would be surprised if anybody living in the twentieth century ever read it.

Offhand, I couldn't think of many literary Ednas. Edna Ferber was a best-selling novelist in the early twentieth century, and Edna O'Brien is doing well in the latter part.

Then there was Edna St. Vincent Millay. In my college days she had been one of my enthusiasms. I liked her poems because many of them were terse — short lines and short poems.

On my bookshelves I have a first edition of *Wine from These Grapes*, published in 1934. I wonder now why I bought it. That was the year I graduated from college, smack in the middle of the Depression, and I had no job or prospect of one. My parents were still supporting me, and I must have used some of my allowance to buy the book. I suppose a kind of post-college nostalgia hit me.

After a glamorous career filled with admiration and honors, the poet's life turned sour. She came to Dayton in the 1940s when she was nearing the age of fifty to give a lecture to the members of the Dayton English Club. We all wore our fanciest hats and dresses to the tea that preceded the lecture.

She had consumed a great amount of gin in her hotel room, and by the time the agitated program chairman was able to steer the poet from her room to the lecture scene, Miss Millay was in an ugly mood.

A striking woman with red hair and wearing a red velvet dress, she rose after the introduction and glared at the microphone.

"I am told," she said in a rasping tone, "that I must speak into this contraption."

She then pushed it aside and began reading.

"We can't hear you," voices in the back of the room called.

She stopped, glared and began again. Then she stopped.

"What is that noise?" she asked.

"It's the air-conditioning system," the president said.

"Let it be turned off!" she shouted, striking a Greek tragedy pose.

The president scurried out, and Miss Millay waited. After a while the throbbing quieted a little, and she started her poem again.

The air conditioning came on again.

"I cannot compete with that," she said and stalked out of the meeting with a somewhat weaving gait.

Two hundred women who had paid two dollars each sat there stunned. The meeting broke up, and gabbling members headed for the elevators.

The one I squeezed into was packed. Somebody near the back announced in a loud voice that she was going to ask for her money back.

Helen Hultman, an English teacher at my school, was on the elevator near the door. She turned and faced the crowd.

"Wouldn't you have considered it a privilege," she asked, "if you could have paid two dollars to see Shelley throw a fit?"

Silence fell in the elevator.

I thought it was a brilliant line, although I don't know that even in her palmiest days Vincent, as she called herself, ranked with Shelley. She was hailed by critics as the leading American woman poet in those days, and many of them compared her favorably with Robert Frost.

Her reputation went into a decline long before she died, and it is hard to say where she ranks now. She has two and one-half columns in Bartlett compared with a little over nine for Frost. In *Modern American Poetry*, published when both poets were living, Louis Untermeyer, the anthologist, gave fourteen pages to Millay and seventeen to Frost. In 1976, however, not a one of her poems was included in *The New Oxford Book of American Verse*.

No matter how delightful some of her poetry is, I felt I couldn't let my cat carry the name of such an eclipsed writer.

Ernest Hemingway named some of his cats for his friends. He had Alice B. Toklas, Gertrude Stein, Agatha Christie, Jeanette MacDonald, and F. Scott Fitzgerald.

Erma Bombeck is my only famous literary friend. Erma used to live in Dayton, and we worked on the same newspaper until she became famous and moved to Paradise Valley, Arizona. I called to ask her if she would like to have a cat named for her.

"I think you should know I have birds," she replied.

"Birds? You do? How many? What are their names?

"Ok, are you ready for this?" she began. "Since the kids are grown and gone, I am down to eight birds. Two are unnamed as they squawk a lot and are living on borrowed time. I used to have two lovebirds and a pair of finches called Bob and Carol and Ted and Alice. Bob ate Carol, I know he did, and he's history. Ted and Alice remain.

"There's a parakeet named Missy and the two un-named birds from my mother. She said, 'If I wanted all that mess, I'd have had more children.'

"The number three resident is Barney, a parrot for whom I bought a cassette so he could sing *Carmen*. The only thing he does is whistle and say 'Telephone,' which drives me nuts. Are you sure you want to do this?"

Well, no. Since Erma is a bird woman, she probably doesn't like cats and might not want one named for her.

I decided to look up what other writers called their cats.

T.S. Eliot in *Old Possum's Book of Practical Cats*

called some of the cats in his poems Jennyanydots, Growltiger, Rum Tum Tugger, Mungojerrie, Rumpel-teazer, Mr. Mistoffelees, Bustopher and Macavity. I didn't care for any of those.

Mark Twain gave most of his cats polysyllabic names like Beelzebub, Blatherskite, Genesis, and Deuterono-my. I couldn't imagine Edna with such a name.

Thomas Hood named a cat Tabitha Longclaws Tiddleywink and her three kittens Pepperpot, Scratch-away, and Sootikins.

Humph!

I glanced over my bookshelves for names of women authors. Dorothy Parker? Anita Loos? Miss Mullock? Helen Santmyer? Barbara Tuchman? Jane Austen? P.D. James? Katharine White? Gertrude Jekyll? Eleanor Perenyi? Marcia Davenport? Ernesta Ballard? Edith Wharton?

Edith. How about Edith? There are a number of literary Ediths — Edith Wharton, Edith Somerville, Edith Sitwell, and Edith Hamilton, to mention four. Then there is Edith with golden hair, the sister of grave Alice and laughing Allegra.

I also have a friend named Edith. She and I exchanged Christmas presents since the days when you could buy something nice for two dollars. Over the years the price we paid for presents rose with inflation to five dollars, to ten, to twenty-five. Now we are at the stage of life where we don't need any more things, so I give her a fifty-dollar bill and she gives me one.

The afternoon I went to SICSA, I had Edith's fifty-dollar bill in my pocketbook and used it to pay the fee for Edna and buy some of her supplies.

Edith it would be.

Edna came into the living room and sat looking out of her window.

I picked her up.

"You are getting a new name," I told her. "From now on, your name is Edith." I made a little mark on her forehead with my finger the way the rector does at church.

"I baptize thee Edith."

I put Edith down, walked to the kitchen, opened the cupboard door, and took out a box of treats called Bonkers. They are little bits of food flavored with chicken or liver.

"Edith!" I called, shaking the box. "Edith!"

Edith came running, tail hoisted and an expectant look on her face. I gave her three Bonkers.

By bedtime Edith had had twelve Bonkers, and I was pretty sure she had learned her new name.

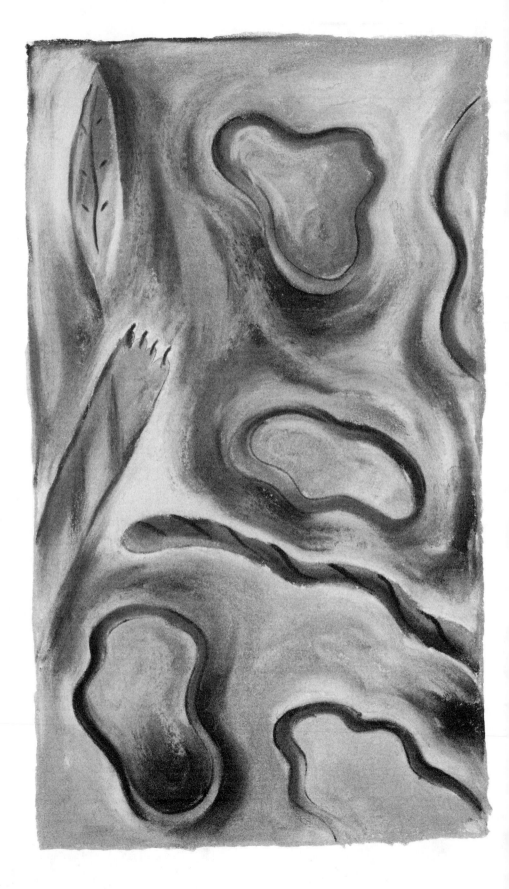

Rubber Bands and a Paw

Edith moved into our house on Saturday. On Sunday morning she discovered how interesting it was to watch water swirl down into the garbage disposer. The best route to the sink was to leap up on my kitchen chair, hop onto the breakfast table, jump a chasm to the stove, and run along the kitchen counter to the sink. Whenever she heard sounds of cooking in the kitchen, she came running, hopping, leaping and jumping, ears standing straight up, tail at the perpendicular and a green gleam of anticipation in her eyes. She sat on the chopping block, curled her tail around her front paws, and waited for the faucet to be turned on. With unwavering concentration she watched plain water going down the drain and bent over studiously to see the soapy water disappear. I have seen graduate students taking final exams with less concentration.

During the day, Edith studied water whenever it went down a drain, whether in the kitchen, the basement, or the bathroom. That evening I filled the tub with warm water, bath bubbles, and me. Edith came into the bathroom, leaped lightly to the tub rim, and sat down to watch. The first time I wiggled my toes at the end of the tub, she tried to catch one, thinking, I suppose, it was a fish. Soon, however, she looked over her shoulder at my head sticking out of the other end of the tub and gave me a look that said, "Those aren't fish. You are doing that."

She paced along the tub rim, studying the bubbles like a scholar's first look at the Dead Sea Scrolls.

She came to a wet spot and slipped.

Nobody ever got in and out of a tub faster than Edith. In a flash she disappeared into the hall, her bubble-bath tail looking like a stick of cotton candy. I leaped out of the tub and grabbed a towel to dry her.

Next day I began to learn that cat people like other cat people. When Virginia, then my editor at the newspaper, found I had acquired a cat, she went out on her lunch hour and bought me a 528-page book, *Cats: Breeds, Care, and Behavior*, by Shirlee A. Kalstone. I skimmed the book as I rode home on the bus. It is amazing all the things there are to learn about nutrition, grooming, health, behavior, breeding, and protection for cats.

When I left the bus at our corner and walked up the hill to the house, I began to worry what Edith had been doing this first time I had left her alone.

I had to grin at myself. I had never worried about my potted plants.

As I put the key into the door between the garage and the laundry room, I heard thumps coming down the steps, thump, thump, thump. I opened the door.

There stood Edith looking up at me with those beautiful chartreuse-gold eyes, a real, live somebody.

"Hello, honey dear," I said.

I think I blushed. I had never called anybody such a sentimental name before.

While I had dinner, I read what Shirlee Kalstone said about correcting bad habits in a cat.

"Just as you praise a cat when it does something right," she said, "so you must discipline it when it misbehaves. And to make a reprimand effective, the cat must be caught in the act because it will not feel guilty about or understand discipline for a misdeed that occurred in the past."

She suggested a firm "No!" accompanied by a loud handclap or slap of a folded newspaper across your palm.

Edith had already formed one bad habit: jumping on the table and running across the stove and counter to see the water come out of the faucet. I ought to nip that habit right away.

After dinner I put the dishes into the sink and turned on the water.

Edith came running from the living room and leaped from chair to table to stove to counter.

"No!" I said and clapped my hands. I lifted her down to the floor.

She crouched low and flattened her ears. In a moment she sat up, gave her chest a few licks, turned, and stalked into the living room, her tail drooping.

I turned on the water again. Tail aloft, she hustled into the kitchen and came to a stop at my feet. She looked up, her chartreuse eyes looking unwinkingly into mine.

"Ow," she said softly, her whole being in her eyes. "Ow."

Still she held my gaze. I could read her mind.

"What harm does it do your counter for me to sit on it and watch the lovely water go down the drain? I'm a clean kitten. I wash my paws every time I eat. Please, please let me see the water."

Breathes there a person who can resist the pleading in a kitten's eyes?

"Oh, all right," I said and lifted her up to the sink.

So much for the first lesson in discipline.

During our first week I made an appointment for Edith to see a veterinarian. On Catherine's recommendation, I chose Dr. Douglas Coatney; he had been the vet for her first cat, Tiger.

Edith shrieked and howled all during the five-mile drive to his office. She hated her cardboard carrying box, and the motion of the car, as I found out before we arrived at the clinic, upset her digestive system. Before I could take her into the office, I had to go inside and ask for some paper towels.

Dr. Coatney is young, fair-haired, and blue-eyed. He has cats of his own, and right off Edith liked his soft voice and gentle way of handling her. She hopped out of her carrying case and looked him over and explored his examining table.

He checked her ears, her eyes, her teeth, and her body. Then he told her he would give her two shots. Edith watched him fill the syringe and looked up into his eyes as he gave her the first shot. She watched him fill the syringe again.

"Edith is very intelligent," he said. "Most cats pay little attention to what the vet is doing, but Edith watches every move I make. What's more, she jumped right out of her box. Most cats have to be pulled out."

My chest swelled.

At the end of the examination he offered her a treat. She sniffed at it but declined.

"She's a little frightened," he said. He told me to bring her back in a month to be spayed and held her carrying case for her to leap into, which she did willingly. He grinned.

"She knows she's going home," he said.

Edith's living room has windows from ceiling to floor. Outside, birds flit from oak to mulberry. Squirrels run across the lawn and, right under her nose, bury acorns in the sweet woodruff bed under the window. Down across the hillside, dogs on leashes walk with their companions, and cars rush up and down the hilly road. Edith's desire from the beginning was to join the living panorama outside the window. She was not, however, allowed to go outside until she had been spayed. That was the agreement with SICSA.

Every time somebody opened the front door or the French doors to the porch, Edith tried to go through. I decided it would be best to come and go through the basement laundry room and the garage.

The garage is an unlovely place. Its floor is cold and dusty concrete. A small room opening off one side holds shelves of empty flower pots, leftover paint, boxes, and bottles of insecticides. Window screens are stacked on one wall along with a copper wash boiler filled with empty mayonnaise jars. The garage has an untidy work-bench, empty bags for shrubbery clippings, cans of driveway salt, bags of fertilizer, trash cans, a snow blower, lawnmower, reels of garden hose, hoes, rakes, and an automobile.

It is a room to pass through as quickly as possible.

To Edith, deprived of the outside world, the garage became her second-most heart's desire.

The cat book warns that garages are dangerous to kittens, who have been known to die from licking anti-freeze spots on the floor.

One morning during our first week when I opened the door to the garage, a brown fur cannonball whizzed between my feet.

"Edith! Come back here! Cats aren't allowed in the garage. Besides, I have to catch the bus."

Hah! What did Edith care about what the cat book says or about bus schedules?

I put down my pocketbook and brief case. It's a large garage and it was five minutes before I found her on the third pot shelf. I carried her squirming into the house. I had missed the bus.

When I went downstairs half an hour later to take the next bus, Edith thump-thump-thumped behind me.

"No!" I said at the door and clapped my hands.

She backed away from the door and crouched with ears flattened.

I felt unhappy as I closed the door. She looked so cowed.

When I came home that afternoon, the window curtains in the laundry room lay on the floor. Upstairs in the living room the jade plant hung upended over the rim of its pot, and a mound of soil made a dark spot on the carpet. I don't know whether she was angry because I scolded her and was paying me back, or whether she had to find some outlet for her kittenish good spirits. I put the curtain back up, pushed the jade plant back into its pot and cleaned up the carpet.

My morning routine is to get out of bed, put on my robe and slippers, and walk into the kitchen. I step onto the scales, read the bad news, then have breakfast.

The third day, Edith began a routine that she still follows, of coming into the bedroom when the alarm goes off, jumping up on the bed, and saying "Ow" into my face. She waits for me to get up and put on my bathrobe and slippers. Then she walks in front of me into the kitchen and sits down on the scales. In the beginning she weighed two pounds.

Next I fill her water and food bowl and while she eats, I open the front door to get the newspaper. It comes with a rubber band around it, and I usually take

off the band and drop it on the table. While I eat breakfast, I read the paper.

Five days after her arrival, Edith walked over to her
food bowl, ate a few bites and walked away.

Something was wrong, for Edith is a prodigious
eater. The book said a cat's nose is supposed to be cool
to the touch. Hers was hot.

Panic set in. I tried to coax her to eat, but she walked
away and curled up in her chair.

I stood looking down at her. How could I go to
work and leave her at home, sick and alone? I thought
of Vivian Jones.

Work be hanged! I'd stay home and as soon as Dr.
Coatney's office opened, I'd be there with Edith.

While I was dressing, I heard a peculiar noise in the
kitchen. Edith crouched flat on the floor, her head
swinging from side to side the way a hose nozzle swings
back and forth on the ground before you turn the water
off. She gave a series of coughs, like small puppy barks.

In a moment she stood up, walked over to her dish
and began eating.

At the spot where she had been crouching lay six
rubber bands. They were warm and wet.

I called Dr. Coatney as soon as his office opened.

"I think she will be all right," he said. "But don't
let her get any more rubber bands. Some cats like to

play with them, but I never knew of any to swallow them before."

He warned not to let anything small such as a threaded needle, a coin, or a small button lie around where Edith could get it.

I was an hour late for work, but I didn't care.

That night when I had finished dinner and sat down to watch the TV evening news, Edith came into the living room and stood looking up at me for a moment. Without any warning and not even a quiver of muscle, she sprang straight up and landed in my lap. She began kneading at my skirt with her paws. Finally she turned around and lay down.

I felt as proud as if I had been made a Dame of the British Empire.

It looked as though Edith and I were getting along together quite well, but I wished she would give some sign that she really liked me.

Sylvia Townsend Warner says in her collected letters that once when she was reading in bed, one of her cats crawled up over the humps and bumps of the bedclothes, looked her straight in the eye and then put a paw on her cheek.

"It was pure affection," Sylvia wrote.

I wished Edith would do something like that, but I had already learned you can't make a cat do anything she doesn't want to do.

On Saturday afternoon, the anniversary of our first week together, I was lying on the sofa reading. I didn't know that Edith was in the room until with a thump she landed on my chest. She began to tread alternately with one front paw and then the other on my stomach. She trampled for about a minute and then settled down in a Sphinx pose. In a little while her eyes closed, her head dropped to one paw, and she began to purr.

I tried holding the book above her back, but it grew heavy and finally I put it on the floor and closed my eyes. We both slept for half an hour.

The book was *Jennie*, by Paul Gallico, a novel about Peter, a boy who turned into a cat, and Jennie, a cat who befriended Peter and taught him the mysteries of being a cat.

Once Peter asked her why sometimes she tramped with her paws before she lay down. (May Sarton in *The Fur Person* calls the action "making starfish.")

"'It has to do with feeling happy,' Jennie said. 'It goes all the way back to our being kittens and being nursed by our mothers. We cannot even see at first, but only feel, for when we are first born we are blind and our eyes open only after a few weeks. But we can feel our way to her breast and bury ourselves in her soft, sweet-smelling fur to find her milk, and when we are there we work our paws gently up and down to help the food we want so much to flow more freely . . . We never forget those moments with our mothers. They remain with us the rest of our lives. And, later on, long after we are grown, when something makes us very happy, our paws and claws go in and out the same way, in memory of those early times of our first real happiness.'"

The evening of our first nap together I was sitting on the sofa watching a television show about lions in Africa. Edith sat on my lap with her forepaws resting on the sofa arm, and her eyes followed the movement of the lions across the screen. My hand lay in my lap.

I felt something soft in my hand. Edith had put her paw in it.

It was as tender a moment as Sylvia T. Warner ever experienced.

Just that morning I had read these lines in a poem by Algernon Charles Swinburne:

> *Stately, kindly lordly friend,*
> *Condescend*
> *Here to sit by me, and turn*
> *Glorious eyes that smile and burn,*
> *Golden eyes, love's lustrous meed,*
> *On the golden page I read.*

All your wondrous wealth of hair,
  Dark and fair,
Silken-shaggy, soft and bright
As the cloud and beams of night,
Pays my reverent hand's caress
Back with friendlier gentleness.

Dogs may fawn on all and some
  As they come;
You, a friend of loftier mind,
Answer friends alone in kind.
Just your foot upon my hand
Softly bids it understand.

When I read those lines, I felt a kinship with Swinburne that a whole college semester of Victorian poets never gave me.

There I sat, thinking about Swinburne, with Edith's paw in my hand until she withdrew it and hopped down to go on an errand of her own.

Something had happened to the person who once thought unkindly about old ladies dotty about their cats or goldfish.

New World

My beige sofa began to look hairy, as if it were sprouting whiskers. One day I surprised Edith standing on her hind legs and scratching away at the sofa with her front claws.

All my cat books — and by now I had a shelf filled with them — say that there are two ways to save the furniture: have the cat declawed or train it to use a scratching post.

One writer on cat behavior says it is worse to remove a cat's claws than to deprive cat owners of their finger-nails.

Scratching is an inherited trait so that cats can remove frayed or worn claws and expose the new claws growing underneath. By repeated scratching they groom themselves, too, removing skin irritations and combing out tangles.

An outdoor cat needs claws to climb out of the reach

of dogs, a rival cat, or a mean person. If ever a cat becomes lost, it needs claws to catch mice or chipmunks for food.

My mother had a few sayings she lived by and required me to observe, too. One was "Save some, give some, spend some." Another was "Always be sure to have something to fall back on." Another was "People are more important than things."

I applied the last one in this situation. Edith is more important than the furniture.

I bought a carpet-covered scratching post and set it in the living room by Edith's window. I took her fawn-colored paws in my fingers and moved them up and down on the post. Then I gave her a Bonkers.

Some cats, I understand, never do learn to use the scratching post. Dr. Coatney told me about a woman whose cat is a patient of his. She has repapered a room three times because her cat shreds the wallpaper.

Edith, thank goodness, is not like that cat. She hooks her claws into the sofa when she stretches after a nap, but she no longer rakes them through the fabric. She does her real scratching outdoors on tree trunks.

I was visiting in the home of Ina Murphy of Cashel, County Tipperary, Ireland, one Christmas. On St. Stephen's Day she went outside to hang up the dish towels, and I heard her shouting and swearing. When

I rushed out to see what had happened, she showed me.

Jemima, her black-and-white cat, had produced six kittens under the stoop during the night.

"I could kill that cat," she muttered, coming back into the house. "This is the sixth litter she has had."

I suggested she should have Jemima spayed.

"You mean have her castrated?" Ina required in a shocked tone. "That would be a mortal sin!"

She said that Jemima had just as much right to lead a normal life as anybody else. No veterinarian in Ireland would think of castrating an animal. He would be excommunicated, she said, if the priest heard about it.

I put the Irish attitude down to the country's being nearly one hundred percent Roman Catholic. I didn't ask Ina what became of all the kittens. She probably drowned them.

The day for Edith's spaying arrived. Dr. Coatney said not to give her food or water the day of the operation because she would have to take a general anesthetic.

She could not understand why her food and water bowls were empty that morning. She sat by my chair and implored me with her beautiful eyes and her soft cries to relent, relent for the love of all creatures great and small.

Her new carrying case had a soft orange towel in the bottom and a screened door so she could see out. When it was time to leave, Edith went into the carrier willingly. She was always ready to crawl into any opening she hadn't seen before.

As I shut the door on her, I felt guilty. She trusted me, and here I was taking her to a strange place where she would have to be caged and given an anesthetic and cut open with a knife. What is more, she would have to stay there overnight.

I was miserable, but she rode along in the car happily enough until we came within a few blocks of the clinic. I think she remembered going that way before when she had her shots. She cried so loudly that I was afraid drivers in other cars would hear her. She refused to be comforted by soothing words and scratchings on the chin. When I opened the clinic door, she let out a tremendous yowl.

Dr. Coatney's office helper took Edith away at once. I drove back home feeling desolate. Oh, how empty the house seemed that night. The potted plants didn't do a bit of good.

My spirits perked up the next day when it was time to call for Edith. She seemed as chipper as before. She hustled into the carrying case without any objection.

At home she hurried out of the carrier and ran up the stairs with as much pep as if she hadn't had a hysterectomy. She crunched her food merrily, her tail stretched out on the floor behind her.

She had a bare spot on her stomach and a row of stitches. Dr. Coatney said that as soon as he took out the stitches, she could go outdoors.

If I had known what I learned later, Edith probably would never have gone outdoors except with me.

The outdoors teems with danger for cats. Hawks and owls have carried off many a kitten. A dog can maul or kill a cat.

Some adults and children take delight in mistreating cats. Automobiles take their toll.

Pesticides, sprays and powders used on lawns to kill insects and weeds can be harmful. If a cat rolls on grass that has been chemically treated and licks his fur, he can die. He can pick up lethal chemicals by drinking from puddles. Once a neighbor was horrified to see Edith drinking from a sprinkling can in which she had dissolved an insecticide harmful to persons and animals.

Then there are fleas to pick up. Fleas cause skin disorders, anemia, liver damage, and tape worms, which Edith has had twice.

As it was, however, I had no idea then that so many dangers lurked outdoors. I love to spend as many hours as I can outdoors gardening, golfing or hiking, and I wanted Edith to have that kind of pleasure, too. Well, not golfing, of course, although, as you will see, she does garden.

A red harness waited for Edith's first day outdoors. I had to read how cats can be trained to walk on a leash, and I planned to teach her to walk with one until she had become familiar with the perimeters of our property, beyond which she was not supposed to venture.

Hah!

When the afternoon of the day for her first trip outdoors arrived, we had a tussle to get the harness on her. She rolled and rolled and squirmed and tried to get out of it. I realize now that I should have had her wear it in the house for a few days to get used to it. My early education in training Edith was a lot of trial and error.

Once it fastened around her chest, I carried her outside and set her down on the top step.

"Now we will walk down the steps," I said.

I stepped down and pulled slightly on the leash. Edith refused to budge. I pulled harder. Edith started backing up. No soft words, no hard tugs, nothing would move her. She dug her claws into the step and there she sat. Nothing in this world can be more determined than a kitten who doesn't want to do what you want her to do.

Finally she hopped off the step onto the grass and sat gazing around her. Then she gave a series of little leaps, scratched at the grass and rolled over.

I sat down on a step and studied how I could get her to walk. We sat for a long time. The telephone rang. I fastened Edith's harness to the railing and went indoors. When I came out five minutes later, the leash dangled from the railing, but it was empty.

Panic set in.

Dorothy happened to be in the kitchen that day cleaning.

"Take the Bonkers box outside and shake it and call her," she suggested. I shook the Bonkers box up and down the steps and all around the yard.

No Edith.

Edith was only eight months old. She wore no collar. She had never been outdoors before and had no way of knowing what a dog or a car or a boy with a rock could do.

I called Catharine.

"Stop worrying," she said. "She will come home. If she hasn't returned by dinnertime, call me again."

How could she possibly find her way home? She had never been outdoors before.

I drove around the block. Edith wasn't in the bushes, on the lawns or in the street.

It was the longest afternoon of my life. The Hundred Years War was but a twinkling. I could not work. I could not read. I could not watch television. What the disappearance of a two-pound package of furry kitten can do to an otherwise sensible woman is remarkable.

Time came to prepare dinner. I didn't care if I never ate another meal.

I sat at the kitchen table, staring out of the window.

Up on the windowsill hopped Edith. She looked at me through the window and opened her mouth in a meow I couldn't hear.

We both ate a whopping dinner.

"You are the most wonderful cat in the world," I told her.

"Ow," said Edith.

The Hunter

While I read on the porch one afternoon and Edith stalked butterflies, a gray squirrel hopped out of a tree and perched on a stone, eating an acorn.

I happened to look up the moment Edith saw him.

She crouched low on the ground and watched, motionless. Then she put one paw forward and then another and inched toward him, ears pointed forward. The squirrel, his back to Edith, seemingly had his entire attention on the acorn.

When Edith crept within two feet of the squirrel, she froze like a statue, the tip of her tail flicking back and forth. She seemed to tense her muscles.

She sprang, her front paws outstretched.

The squirrel leaped, wheeled and ran for the nearest tree, and Edith scampered behind him. Up the oak trunk he went. Edith ran after him.

By the time she reached the first limb, the squirrel had disappeared into the leafy canopy above.

Edith backed part of the way down the trunk, turned and finished the trip headfirst. Then she sat down and gazed up into the tree.

With patience she waited for the squirrel to come down. Twenty minutes passed before she decided that she really didn't want that squirrel anyhow.

She gave herself a good washing and stalked off.

As far as I know she never chased a squirrel again.

One day shortly afterwards I saw her coming up the steps to the porch. She looked as if she had sprouted a mustache.

As she came nearer, I saw she carried something in her mouth. Before I could close the door, she sped past me through the entrance hallway, through the dining room and into the bathroom. Holding her head high, she leaped into the bathtub.

She laid her catch on the cold porcelain — a baby chipmunk.

Horrified, I stared into the tub. Like many another woman, I would rather face a lion in the jungle than a bat or a mouse in the house. I wouldn't climb on a chair to get away from a mouse, but a bat swooping through the living room can unnerve me.

I remember once before I was married, the love of

my life and I were sitting in the living room looking at television. A bat flew through the room.

"Good," I thought. "there's a big, six-foot stalwart man here, and he will get the bat out for me."

The bat flew through the room again.

"I think I'd better be going home," said Bill and stood up.

"You wouldn't go home and leave me to face this bat!"

He had every intention of doing so.

For a moment I considered breaking the engagement. What's the use of having a man around the house if he won't help get a bat out of it?

He did help, although reluctantly.

I thought about the bat as I stood looking at the chipmunk. This time there was nobody but me to deal with the problem.

The poor thing was just a baby. It did not even have its eyes open. Edith pawed at it and looked up at me, pride on every whisker.

I felt appalled at this evidence of Edith's feral nature.

Cats are predators, of course, and their mothers teach them techniques of stalking and capturing prey. Books about cat behavior have long lists of delicacies cats like: mice, rats, chipmunks, moles, shrews, birds, butterflies, moths, grasshoppers, crickets, lizards, and toads. Sometimes they eat their kill, and sometimes they bring them home as gifts. Anyone who receives a gift from a kitten or cat should praise the donor and dispose of the gift privately.

I patted Edith and thanked her and told her she is a wonderful cat.

I do think she is wonderful, because she put the chipmunk in the bathtub where it could not escape. One of my friends has a cat who brings chipmunks and field mice in through a cat door and lets them escape under the washer.

I picked the little creature up on a pancake turner and carried it outdoors to the hillside, Edith walking beside me, her head high.

Since that day I have found many a chipmunk corpse on the lawn, testimony to her prowess. Once I found something much worse, but that is a story for later.

On second thought, I think I will tell it now.

Some authors hint at great revelations to come and then forget all about it. I have lived long enough to observe that hinting is a kind of teasing, and teasing is a mean trick. People who tease get a kick out of the other person's discomfiture or befuddlement, and I think that is downright nasty.

Before we get to what I found on the lawn, we need to talk about Edith's weight problem. On one visit to the vet Dr. Coatney pointed out that among other diseases obesity can bring on congestive heart failure, respiratory troubles, indigestion, constipation, flatulence, kidney disease, diabetes mellitus, susceptibility to viral and bacterial infections, and osteoarthritis.

He then reported that Edith weighed thirteen pounds but should weight no more than ten. Calling on almost forgotten mathematical skills, I figured by proportion that if at one hundred and forty pounds I were as overweight as Edith, I would weight one hundred eighty-two. That's as much as a heavyweight boxer.

That did it.

Edith would have to go on a diet.

Dr. Coatney said to measure out what Edith should have for a day and give her half in the morning and half in the evening.

Edith, however, likes small meals and many of them. Every time she returns from a sally outdoors, she heads straight for her dish. I cannot bear to see her disappointed. That is, to be sure, how she became obese in the first place.

Most cats are like Edith in that they prefer many small meals. After all, one mouse is quite small. I decided to give Edith one mouseworth of food several times a day.

The new system worked well — I thought. Whenever she came back into the house, she headed for the bowl, ate what was there and did not complain.

The needle on the scale began to edge downward to the twelve mark.

One day I gave her a mouseworth of beef for lunch. She ate it all, licked the bowl and went out to patrol the garden.

Not long afterwards I saw her *couchant* in the grass. Every now and then her head dipped earthward and when she lifted it, she seemed to be chewing.

Some of my friends dislike cats because they catch and eat birds. Yet most of us have no qualms about eating lamb, pork, beef, veal, or chicken although we know what goes on in slaughterhouses.

Edith has caught many a chipmunk in our garden. She plays with her catch, letting it run away from her and scampering after it to catch it again. Sometimes it escapes into the ivy or a crevice in a stone wall. Sometimes it doesn't, and I later find a corpse on the lawn.

This time was different.

After a while she stood up and walked over to the top of the steps. She gave herself a good washing.

I went out into the yard to the spot where she had been lying. I found a chipmunk head.

Nothing else remained. She had eaten paws, skin, tail and all.

A fig, says Edith, for diets.

Jailed

Lewis and Catharine wanted to spend a week's vacation in Florida and asked if Blackwell might visit Edith while they were gone. The two cats knew each other; sometimes Blackwell came along when the Bookers visited me at my house, and sometimes I took Edith along when I called on them.

I thought we might have a little problem when Blackwell's visit was for more than an afternoon, and so I explained to Edith that Blackwell was coming to visit, that she was not going to stay forever and that she must be kind and polite to the visitor.

Edith seemed to listen to the explanation. Then she looked away as if thinking it over and walked to the window to check on the hillside activities.

Not long afterwards Blackwell, accompanied by food, dishes, and litter box, arrived at the house.

Lewis and Catharine left right away. Blackwell

watched them go. Then she walked into the living room, picked out a chair, hopped into it, and closed her eyes.

After a while Edith came into the room and saw Blackwell in her very own private chair. She went into her jungle crouch.

She exploded into the air and landed on Blackwell, who socked Edith four rapid right paws to the jaw. Edith flopped on her side, brought up her back feet and hit Blackwell back. Both cats rose on their hind feet, grabbed with their front paws and bit each other in the throat, growling all the while.

I picked Edith up. She squirmed and twisted in my grasp, her eyes fastened on Blackwell.

"Let me at her! Put me down!" Edith seemed to shout.

I took her to the kitchen and set her on the table.

"Now you look here, Edith," I said, holding her by the scruff of her neck. "Blackwell is your guest and gets to choose first. If she wants to sleep in your chair, there are plenty of other chairs for you to sleep in. You must be polite. If there is any more growling or picking on her at all, I will punish you."

I sent the cats outdoors to work off their energy, and when they came back, all was peace for a time.

We had a domestic scene in the living room that evening. I read a book, Blackwell lay on the floor beside

Edith's scratching post and Edith lay on the other side of the post.

Without the least warning, Edith bit Blackwell's tail. Blackwell rose, jabbed Edith in the jaw, and gave her a bear hug. The fight was on.

"That's it," I said to Edith, grabbing her up. "I warned you."

In the basement is a room as large as the living room. In it I keep extra furniture and stacks of empty cartons that might come in handy some day.

I took Edith's food and water dish and litter box into that room. Then I took her down, told her she was in jail until she could behave better, and shut the door.

Two hours later I went downstairs to see how Edith was faring. She had gone to sleep in one of the empty cartons. I told her if she was ready to treat Blackwell right, she could come upstairs any time.

Edith stood up, yawned, and stretched. I left the door open.

After a little while Edith walked into the living room. Blackwell lay asleep in Edith's chair. Edith hopped up and wiggled until Blackwell moved over and made room for her.

We all watched a TV program about some fish swimming in a lagoon.

By the time the show ended, Blackwell had gone to sleep, but Edith had disappeared. She had not reappeared three hours later when I looked for her to say goodnight.

On previous occasions when she was missing for more than two hours, I had found her shut up in the broom closet, another time in the linen shelves, and one time in the drawer where the telephone book is.

She wasn't in any of those.

It is disconcerting when a cat disappears in the house. I remember reading about Francis Wells of Sheffield, England, who found, when he removed his laundry from the washer, the unconscious and wet body of his cat, Zadok. He wrapped Zadok in a warm towel and put her by the fire. She soon revived and seemed none the worse for her wash and rinse. Wells said he was glad the washer was set for gentle wash and slow spin.

George Freedley, founder and librarian for thirty years of the theatre collection of the New York Public Library and author of numerous books on the theatre, wrote two little books in the 1960s about Mr. Cat, a Persian with whom George lived in a New York apartment on East 55th Street.

One day Mr. Cat did not appear for his lunch, nor did he show up the rest of the day. George thought he was around the apartment building somewhere and alerted the doorman, all his neighbors, and the janitor. He conducted a thorough search of the halls, the basement, the roof, everywhere.

Mr. Cat was wearing an identification collar and harness. George fully expected somebody to call. When no one did, he put an ad in the newspaper and called the ASPCA.

Another day went by, and George became frantic. He wrote out a description of Mr. Cat and gave his telephone number at home and at his office. He offered a reward and put copies of his notice in all the mailboxes in his apartment house and in the neighboring ones.

He heard nothing, but a woman who saw his ad in the paper said she thought she had seen a cat wandering around Beekman Place. George rushed over and left notices in all the mailboxes.

Toward the end of the fifth week after George had given up all hope, a man called and asked if George had lost a cat. "Oh, yes, yes, yes. Have you found him?"

"No," the caller replied, "but I found a collar with your name and telephone number on it."

The caller told him where to come. George grabbed Mr. Cat's favorite toy, a flashlight, and his carrying case and hurried around to the address, which turned out to be a manufacturing building.

The building was being air-conditioned. In one of the offices workmen had put down a plywood board to cover a hole they made in the floor. When the superintendent, the man who called, took up the board because workmen were about to lay a new floor, he found Mr. Cat's harness and collar.

George got down on the floor and looked into the hole. He called.

He heard a weak mew.

He dropped Mr. Cat's favorite toy into the hole and after a while Mr. Cat crawled to where George could see him in the flashlight beam. George jiggled the toy up and down in the hole and slowly Mr. Cat crawled to where George could reach down and pick him up. He was appalled at how thin Mr. Cat had become.

He carried him home and fixed him a bowl of warm milk. But Mr. Cat had forgotten how to eat. George dipped his fingers in the milk and after a little coaxing, Mr. Cat licked George's fingers. George fed him every two hours all night.

In a few weeks Mr. Cat was as good as ever. He weighed fifteen pounds when he disappeared and one pound when George found him.

It seems impossible that Mr. Cat could have survived almost six weeks without food and water. Dr. Coatney said he thinks two weeks is about as long as he could have lived.

But then I heard about Thomas Cadillac.

One morning on the docks in Sydney, Australia, workmen uncrated a Cadillac that had come by freighter from Detroit. It had been seven weeks in the hold of the ship.

Before the car agency manager attempted to start the car, he opened the hood. Stretched out in the V-shaped space formed by the eight cylinders lay the body of a cat. It evidently had been black, but it had lost most of its fur.

A workman laid it on the dock and began to pick up the crating lumber. He thought he heard a noise coming from the body. He knelt down and inspected the cat carefully. It was breathing faintly.

One of the men rushed the cat to the veterinary. The cat responded to his treatment and in a few weeks he was a fine, strong black cat. The vet named him Thomas Cadillac.

The story of the stowaway, who must have climbed into the car in Detroit before it was crated, appeared in the Sydney newspaper.

Mrs. Clifford G. Poole, wife of an American car dealer in Sydney, offered to adopt Thomas. Because the cat was deemed to be an American citizen, she was required to put up a $500 bond; the American consul signed the papers.

The Australian immigration officer in Sydney read about Thomas. Since Australia had laws that no livestock could be imported into the country, he ruled that Thomas would have to be sent back to the United States.

The Pooles, who were from Detroit, booked passage to take Thomas home. This time he traveled in a stateroom with all the food he could eat, supplied by the ship's cook.

Wire services picked up the story, and when the ship docked in Honolulu, eleven photographers from newspapers and motion picture news reels — this happened in 1921, long before television — came aboard to take his picture.

The same thing happened in San Francisco.

Officials of the Cadillac Motor Car Company met the train in Detroit, and Thomas received a jolly welcome. He was given a home in the Cadillac factory and lived there the rest of his days.

Everywhere people wanted to know how a cat could have lived seven weeks in the car engine. Workmen found that every bit of lubricant on the engine parts had been licked dry, and half a booklet of instructions had disappeared.

Whenever Edith disappears in the house or anywhere outside, I think about Mr. Cat and Thomas Cadillac.

I could not find Edith anywhere. I looked under every bed, cupboard, and sofa.

I looked into all the closets and drawers.

My last task before bed is to take the day's collection of newspapers and junk mail to the basement.

While I was down there, something made me look into the room where I had jailed Edith earlier.

Edith hadn't understood that I put her in the basement for punishment. She had gone back to jail and turned in for the night.

Next afternoon Blackwell lay asleep in Edith's chair. This time she lay on her back with her paws in the air.

Edith jumped up on the chair and looked at Blackwell, who never moved. She flopped down in front of Blackwell, her tail to Blackwell's head.

After a while Blackwell woke. Out came her tongue and began licking Edith. She must have hit a sensitive spot, for Edith rose, whirled around, smote Blackwell in the jaw with a right and a left, and lay down again.

When Lewis and Catharine came to take Blackwell home, Edith didn't even say goodbye. For several days afterwards, however, she stalked around the house looking somewhat forlorn.

Another black cat, an ancient gentleman named Moonbeam, lived across the street. Several times from her window, Edith had seen him walking in her yard and she had bristled. When she bristles, she growls and her tail switches back and forth.

One morning as soon as her breakfast was over, she told me she wanted to go out. It was still dark. I opened the door.

She stopped in her tracks on the threshold. Then she backed into the room.

"What's wrong? Changed your mind?"

I went back to my coffee and the newspaper. In a little while I felt Edith's paw on my leg.

"All right."

Once again she froze in the doorway and backed inside. I couldn't see anything in the darkness.

Five minutes later we tried again with the same result. I turned on the porch light.

"That's Moonbeam on the porch," I told her. "You don't need to be afraid of him. Go on out."

She didn't budge. Neither did Moonbeam.

I put a little of Edith's food on a saucer and set it against the porch wall away from the door. Moonbeam bent over it, and Edith stalked past him and down the steps.

After that Moonbeam came every morning. I always

gave him a little food. He was so afflicted with arthritis that it was difficult for him to crouch to his food, so he ate standing up.

One morning I forgot to fill his bowl and went to the door two hours later, he was still waiting.

Another morning he was not on the porch when I opened the door. I left his bowl empty. Five minutes later Edith hopped up on the windowsill.

"You certainly didn't stay long this morning," I said, holding the door for her. But she didn't want to come in.

Then in the darkness I saw the still darker figure of Moonbeam.

I picked up his bowl and took it into the house. When I came back, Moonbeam was waiting, but Edith had gone, her good deed done for the day.

Fleas and Virus

Whenever I come into the house, I look Edith up and speak to her. She greets me in return. Whenever I leave, I tell her where I am going and how long I will be gone.

I don't know how much she understands, but I know it is more than most people might think she does. When two or more of us talk about her, she looks at us and twitches the end of her tail. When she wants attention, she comes and puts her paw on my leg.

"What do you want, Edith?" I ask. "Show me what you want."

She leads me to the food bowl or the front door. A serving table stands in the kitchen between the breakfast table and Edith's food bowl. If she wants food, she walks between the table and the bowl. If she wants to go out, she walks between the two tables.

Grace Pond and Angela Sayer in *The Intelligent Cat*

say that an ordinary cat will sit at a door and call to be let in. Even if it is raining, the cat will still sit there, calling and getting wet.

Judging by that, Edith is no ordinary cat. If she wants to come in, she hops up on the kitchen windowsill and says, "Ow." When she sees me start for the door, she hops down and meets me there. If she doesn't see me, she walks around to every window until she finds me.

She has learned that there is a connection between the scales and food. If her dish is empty and she wants it filled, she sits on the scales until I notice her.

Oftentimes on Thursdays when Dorothy comes to clean our house, she will come into the office or wherever I am working.

"Edith is sitting on the scales again," she says.

Intelligent cats, say Pond and Sayer, have a way of showing when food is unacceptable. They sniff the food and then with one paw they will heap imaginary dirt to cover it.

Once in a long while Edith indicates her opinion of something unpalatable by throwing imaginary dirt over it, but one time she went a little far.

The telephone rang just as I put my dinner plate on the table. As I stood talking, Edith hopped up on the table and sniffed at my pot roast, scalloped cabbage and cottage cheese. Then she pawed at the table cloth and tossed make-believe dirt on it.

Most of my friends like Edith. She likes them, too. If she is outdoors when they come, she generally accompanies them up the front steps. If she is in the house, she greets each one of them with an "Ow."

She particularly likes Dorothy and Millie because they know where her treat box is and give her a little something when they arrive.

Edith knows when Dorothy is coming because that is the time I set out the trash cans. She sits in the driveway and looks down the hill. As soon as she sees Dorothy coming, she runs to meet her, follows her into the house, and goes straight to the cupboard where the treats are. Dorothy always pets her and then gives her three little treats.

One day when Millie came, she held the treats in her hand for Edith to eat.

Edith had her treats and walked away.

"What's the matter, Edith?" Millie asked, holding out her hand. "Don't you want this one?"

Edith kept on walking.

"That's funny," said Millie. "She didn't eat them all."

"How many did you give her?"

"Four."

"She's allowed to have only three."

That's how we found out Edith had learned to count.

Every morning after breakfast, Edith likes to have her head and chin brushed, her back and sides and stomach. After the brushing, she goes outside for her morning tour.

One late summer morning when I finished combing her, I saw a black speck on the comb. I dashed for the cat book.

"If in the combings you find little black specks that don't move," the book said, "they are the excreta of fleas."

I was appalled.

If there was anything in this world my mother taught me was sin, it was bugs of any kind in the house. One morning she found an insect corpse on the windowsill of the guest room. She told us at breakfast that we had bedbugs in the guest room.

She made my father take the bed apart and haul the mattress outdoors, where she gave it a good thumping with the carpet beater. We had to wash the woodwork and all the furniture with some kind of evil-smelling liquid she got at the hardware store. She aired and beat all the rugs.

It took all day for us to get the room back to rights. The next day she found another bug. My father went to look at it.

"Is that the same kind of bug you saw yesterday?" he asked.

She nodded.

"There must be a screen loose somewhere," he said. "That's a June bug and perfectly harmless."

When I called Dr. Coatney for an appointment, the secretary wanted to know what was wrong with Edith. I told her it was the kind of thing one doesn't mention over the telephone.

Our appointment wasn't until eleven o'clock three days later. Edith had to do without breakfast that morning because she sometimes has motion sickness. She wasn't allowed to go outside because she might not come back in time.

We had a stormy morning. Edith searched my eyes with her chartreuse ones, pleading. She sat by the front door and cried.

She cried all the way to the animal clinic.

When it was her turn, I set her carrying case on Dr. Coatney's table. He opened the cage door.

"Will you come out, Edith?" he asked. Edith walked halfway out of the cage and froze.

"That's very good," he said, picking her up. "Most cats will not come out at all. The only time we have no trouble is getting them to go back into the carriers. They know then they're going home."

I felt proud.

He examined her eyes, her ears, and her teeth.

"She seems to be fine," he said. "I'll weigh her for the record."

At that time she weighed eight and a half pounds.

He clipped her claws.

I looked around the room. Nobody was listening.

"I think Edith has fleas."

He laughed.

"So that's it. We were wondering. Not to worry. They're bad this year."

He examined her fur on the top of her back near her tail. Then he checked around her mouth.

"Yes, I think she has picked up some fleas. Any outdoors cat is likely to get them."

He brought out a can of flea powder and said to dust her with it every other day for three weeks. He also suggested running the vacuum sweeper over all the places she snoozes.

That was all there was to it. I had supposed he would dip her in some kind of lethal (to fleas) bath.

Dr. Coatney said she would not need to come back until it was time for her next shot, but the very next week we had to go back to him.

Whenever Edith and I walk up the stairs together, she runs ahead and is sitting by the door before I have gone halfway up.

One Friday night she did not run up the steps. She crawled up. The next morning she rose when I did, walked into the kitchen, sat on the scales, watched me put food into her dish and walked with me when I set the dish down. But she didn't eat one bite.

She walked into the living room and curled into a ball in her favorite chair. She was still there two hours later.

"Edith, what's wrong?" I asked. "Why don't you eat or go out to play?"

Edith looked at me, closed her eyes and let her head drop down on her paw.

I pulled my cat care book off the shelf.

"A change in appetite or behavior, a change in gait or a fever are signs of a sick cat," said the book. She had both a change in gait and appetite. I felt her nose and fur. Both seemed hot to the touch.

"I think you're sick, Edith," I told her. "When Dr. Coatney's office opens in two hours, we're going to be there."

She lay listlessly in her carrying cage and made little weak cries as we drove to the clinic. Dr. Coatney said that her ears were all right and her eyes looked clear. Her mouth was all right. The next thing was to take her temperature.

He showed her the thermometer. She cringed as he inserted it.

When he looked at the thermometer, his eyebrows shot up.

"She's sick, all right. It's 103.6. That's very high for a cat. Now let's find out what's wrong."

He poked her here and there.

"She is flatulent," he said. "She has picked up a virus somewhere. I'll give her a couple of antibiotic shots and put her on medication for three days. That ought to fix her up fine."

Edith howled when he gave her the shots, one in each hip.

"Now," he said. "Do you want to give her pills or liquid medicine?"

"Gee," I replied. "Which is easier?"

"Liquid. It's hard to get cats to take pills, and sometimes they wait until you are not looking and spit them out."

He brought a bottle and a medicine dropper and showed me how to tip up her head, put the dropper in the corner of her mouth, squeeze out the medicine, and hold her head back until she swallowed. He said to give her five milligrams four times a day starting that night and continuing until the medicine was gone. It was citrus-flavored and doesn't taste bad. She was to stay indoors until she was well — probably Monday night. The virus was communicable and, besides, when cats are sick, they creep off into a culvert or somewhere and if you can't find them to give them medication, they will die.

"You did right to bring her in this morning," he said. "Monday might have been too late. I think she looks as if she may throw up on the way home."

He was right.

I resolved right that if ever Edith seemed even a little bit sick, to Dr. Coatney she would go.

Back at home Edith went to bed. She slept all afternoon. I tiptoed around the house and didn't turn on the television for fear I'd disturb her. I picked her a bouquet of petunias and sat with a book by her chair all afternoon.

She didn't eat or drink all day. The cat book says cats must not become dehydrated and the way to check whether they are is to pinch the skin along the back. The pinch should go back into place immediately.

I pinched Edith's fur along her back. She was not dehydrated.

I cooked a chicken and made her a little broth.

She drank a bit of it for her supper.

After supper I put her up on the table and got the medicine bottle, anticipating trouble. I tipped up her head, squeezed the dropper until all the pink medicine disappeared and watched her swallow. She smacked her lips afterwards and eyed the bottle.

Sunday morning Edith ate a good breakfast. I didn't even have to hold her at all when I gave her the medicine.

All my explanations about why she had to stay indoors made no impression on her. Every fifteen minutes she begged to go out.

I had planned to stay home with Edith all day Sunday, but she seemed so much better and was so pesky about wanting to go out that I went to church and left her in the house.

It was a hot day and I left the air conditioning running so she would be cool.

The next day she was out ranging the hill, as good as new.

Missing

Before Edith came, I took vacation trips once or twice a year. I arranged for someone — usually Catharine — to water the plants and check to see that nothing was leaking in the house.

I had planned a trip to Ireland before Edith moved into our house. As time neared for the trip, I discovered the pleasure of anticipation I usually felt had disappeared.

The reason was that lively little soft, furry Edith.

Catharine and Lewis would take her into their home, and Blackwell would be there for her to scrap and play with. But I felt she would be unhappy away from her home, her woods, her jungle at the foot of the lot, her hill, and her street.

Every time I leave the house even to go downtown or to the postoffice or grocery, I feel apprehensive about leaving Edith. If she is in the house, she will clean out her food dish and then take a nap until I come back. I can be reasonably certain she will be safe.

When I back the car out of the garage and she is outdoors, she stands in the yard or sits in the street and watches me drive away. She looks so small. I know that she will wait for me to come back. She recognizes the sound of my car, and often when I drive into the garage, she comes running. But always at the back of my head is the nagging thought that she might run out in front of a car or a mean dog might roam through the neighborhood while I am gone.

The time came when I had to tell her I was going away for two weeks. I felt so guilty I wished I had not planned to go to Ireland. If I had known what was going to happen, I would have canceled the trip right then.

I felt even more miserable when I laid the opened suitcases on the dining room table. Edith came running and leaping. Oh, joy! Something new to explore had appeared. She sniffed at every inch of those suitcases and tried them out as beds. She inspected what went into them: the stockings, blouses, sweaters, skirts. She took naps on the sweaters.

The night before I was to leave I packed a basket with Edith's food and dishes, her comb and brush, an extra collar and several toys. Then I fetched her carrying case and opened the door.

She didn't want to go into the case.

When cajolery wouldn't work, I pointed her in the right direction and gave her a little push. I felt like a traitor.

She cried all the way to Blackwell's house.

Once there she checked out Blackwell's food bar and then went to sleep in the best wing chair.

"We won't tell you if anything goes wrong," Catharine said as I got up to leave. "It's no use to spoil your trip."

I felt worse than ever.

It was a long night at our house after I kissed Edith goodbye and drove back home. No little furry body wound round my legs while I washed the dishes.

Nobody landed on the bed in the middle of the night. No little voices said "Ow" in my ear when the alarm went off in the morning.

When Edith visits Blackwell, the cats spend much of the time on the wooded hill behind the house. It has chipmunks and squirrels and stacks of piled-up logs to climb on. Whenever they want to come back into the house for food or just to be sure everything is all right, they hop up on the kitchen windowsill or go to the glass door that opens on the patio. Lewis or Catharine lets them in.

Catharine said later that after I left, Edith moped

for two days. She refused her food and wouldn't even go outdoors. But on the third day she perked up, ate out of Blackwell's bowl and hers, too, and followed Blackwell out to the hillside.

Toward the end of the first week Catharine left town for a few days. While she was gone, the plan was for Lewis to put the girls outside while he went to the office for the day. He would leave food and water for them in the open garage. When he came home at dinnertime, he and the cats would spend the evening and night together.

Catharine left on Wednesday evening. Thursday morning Lewis fed the cats and turned them out on the hillside.

When he came home about dinnertime that evening, only one cat was waiting for him.

"Where's Edith?" he asked Blackwell.

He called her a few times, but she did not come. He felt sure she would turn up some time during the evening.

She had not returned when darkness settled over Hadley Road. Every time a commercial came on TV, Lewis went to the door and called. He waited up for her until midnight. Then he turned out the lights and went to bed.

"Surely she will be waiting outside in the morning," he said to Blackwell.

The minute he awoke on Friday morning, he ran downstairs to look for Edith.

She was not there.

Oakwood, where Lewis and Catharine live, has a cat ordinance. Cats are required to stay in their own yards. If they are caught wandering about the village, a cat-control officer can pick them up, impound them, and charge their owners a hefty fine.

Lewis called the police department and reported that Edith, a brown and orange tabby wearing a collar with his telephone number, had wandered away. The officer said that if she was picked up, he would notify Lewis.

In the middle of the morning the telephone rang. Lewis jumped to answer the call. A police officer had found a declawed tabby cat.

"No," said Lewis, "Edith has her claws."

He drove all around the streets near the house. Edith did not answer his calls.

He spent another uneasy night.

She had not returned when he opened the door Saturday morning.

Toward dinnertime that night the thought occurred to him that maybe she had taken it into her head to go home. He thought it was unlikely, but he was so worried he wanted to look everywhere he could think of. The two miles from his home to ours is a twisting road through wooded parkland. He didn't see how she could find her way home since the only times she had been at Blackwell's home, she had come in her carrying case in the car. But it was worth a try.

The trip was in vain. No Edith lay on the porch, under the bushes, or on the stone wall.

"Maybe she will be at home when I get back," Lewis thought. But she was not.

He couldn't enjoy the evening. So far as he knew, Edith hadn't had anything to eat for two days. Had she been hit by a car? Was she lying injured somewhere?

Dark came again, and still no Edith. Lewis took a flashlight and searched the bushes in his and the neighbors' yards. He called and called. Feeling miserable, he went to bed. He didn't sleep well.

Sunday morning when he opened the door to let Blackwell out, there on the back step sat Edith. She walked in, rushed to the food bar and ate a whopping meal. Then she walked into the living room, hopped into the very best wing chair in the house, and closed her eyes.

She slept all day.

Next morning she went out with Blackwell, and when Lewis came home that evening, she was there waiting. When Catharine came home several days later, the two cats played on the hillside, dashed into the house for snacks and out again, chased each other through the house at night, engaged in a few feline altercations and in general settled down to a comfortable life.

As for me I had a pretty good time on my trip to Ireland, but I often found myself thinking about Edith and worrying. When it was time to go home, I was glad because I would soon be with that little furry person.

When I arrived home, I didn't even wait long enough to unpack. I left the suitcases in the basement, jumped into the car and drove up to the Booker home.

I parked, walked to the front porch and rang the bell. Around the corner Edith came running, her tail a striped flagpole.

"Ow," she said and rubbed against my legs. I scooped her up and hugged her.

When a little later I opened the door to her carrying case, she didn't have to be pushed. In she went. She was going home.

Every now and then since Edith came, I had written a bit in my newspaper column about Edith's adventures.

I wrote how Edith had disappeared from the Booker home.

When the column appeared, a woman who lives several blocks away called to say she had seen Edith trudging along Adirondack Trail towards our house.

Then Willa, my next-door neighbor called. She had been working in her garden on Friday and filled a bucket with water into which she had dropped some insecticide to spray on a diseased euonymous.

She dashed into the house for something and looking out the window, she saw Edith drinking out of the bucket. Willa ran outside and grabbed her.

"You mustn't drink that, Edith," she told her. "Here. I'll get you some fresh water." She said Edith seemed extremely thirsty and drank and drank and drank. While Edith was drinking, Willa read the label on the insecticide bottle. To her horror she found a warning that the contents were poisonous to people and animals. She didn't know how much Edith had drunk of the poisoned water, but she wasn't going to take any chances. She dashed into the house and called the poison control office.

"The woman who answered was very nice," Willa said. "She didn't seem to mind at all that I was calling about a cat instead of a child. She looked up the poison and said that she thought as long as Edith had plenty of pure water afterwards, she would be all right. She said she might have a sore mouth or tongue for a while."

After Edith finished drinking, she hung around for a long time while Willa worked with the plants. When

Willa finished and went into the house, Edith tried to go along with her.

"I didn't let her come in," said Willa. "I told her she ought to go home. I didn't know you were not there. When I think how Edith came to me for help and I turned her away, I could cry. Don't you ever go away again without letting me know."

I don't know how Edith found her way to our house from the Booker house. She had made the trip several times in the car in her cage, but she couldn't even see out. What is even more remarkable is that when she found I was not at home and Willa wouldn't let her in, she walked all the way back to the Bookers.

When my friends read in the paper about Edith's remarkable exploit, some of them said they thought I had made the story up. They didn't believe she could have found her way home and back again.

Cat literature, however, is filled with tales of cats' remarkable homing instinct.

The Kales family in Virginia gave a cat to some friends who lived in the District of Columbia. After three weeks he disappeared. One week later he turned up at the Kales home, having crossed the Potomac River, whether by bridge or by swimming he never said.

The Hobbs family of Kokomo, Indiana, shipped a cat named Tom by train to Augusta, Georgia, to live with one branch of the family that had moved there. Three weeks after his arrival, he disappeared. Three weeks later Tom returned to his old home in Kokomo, having traveled on foot 721 miles.

Mrs. Robert Landmark moved from Dunkirk, New York, to Denver, Colorado, in May, leaving behind with relatives her pregnant cat, Clementine.

Clementine's kittens were born, trained, and finally weaned. Then Clementine disappeared.

In September Clementine appeared at the Landmark home in Denver, sixteen hundred miles away.

Mr. and Mrs. Arthur Mayer of Evansville, Indiana, moved to another part of town, leaving their cat, Fluffy, with the new tenants of their old home.

Before settling in their new home they went to a resort in Maine and took a second-floor room. One evening Mr. Mayer heard unusual noises outside his bedroom window. When he looked out he found Fluffy trying to crawl up the drainpipe that passed close by his window.

Mrs. Charles B. Smith was working in the kitchen of her home in San Gabriel, California, when she heard a cat mewing at the back door. Looking up at her was a thin gray-and-black cat.

"My, you look tired and hungry," she said. "Just a minute and I'll get you some food."

Aggie, the Smith Scotty, who hated cats, came bar-
reling around the corner of the house. Before Mrs. Smith
could grab the cat, Aggie skidded to a stop, sniffed at
him, touched noses, and began running around in cir-
cles, barking and frisking like a puppy.

Mrs. Smith stared at the cat.

"Tom? Are you Tom? You can't be Tom."

The Smiths had moved to California two years before
from St. Petersburg, Florida. When they moved, they
took Aggie with them, but they left their gray-and-black
cat Tom with the new owners.

Two weeks after they moved, the new owner wrote
that Tom had disappeared.

Two years later Tom arrived at the Smith home,
having trudged three thousand miles across the United
States.

There was no doubt that the cat was really Tom and
not some stray that looked like him. When Mrs. Smith
let him inside, Tom toured the house, rubbing against
every piece of furniture they had brought with them
from St. Petersburg but paying no attention to new
pieces they had bought in California. He ignored the
new baby, born in California, but devoted himself to
Aggie. When Mr. Smith came home that night from
work, Tom ran to meet him.

How Tom managed to find his way across the country and locate the very town, street and house in which his people lived is a phenomenon. Hattie Gray Baker, who reported all these stories in her *195 Cat Tales*, says that cats in common with many other animals possess an ability to tune in on magnetic currents or wave lengths. Homing pigeons possess to a remarkable degree the same ability.

I accept Miss Baker's word that all the stories have been verified.

Knowing Edith, I would be afraid to move to England, say, and leave her here. She would likely try to swim the Atlantic.

Of course, I would never ever even think of moving anywhere without Edith.

Edith's Three W's

Journalists have five W's: Who, what, when, where, why. Edith has three: Walks, water, and washing.

Phyllis, Shirley, Willa, and I regularly go walking every weekday. We try to cover two miles in half an hour.

One morning the four of us started up Springhill and turned into Adirondack Trail. Something caused Willa to turn around.

"Oh, uh," she said. "We have been joined by somebody."

There came Edith, running after us with a determined look on her face.

It was too late to take her back home.

On we walked past piles of brushwood stacked up since the last storm. Every now and then we looked around. Edith still followed.

At almost quarter of a mile from home, we came to a Y in the road. We took the right fork into Willowgrove and started downhill. Phyllis stopped and held up her hand.

"Listen."

A wail rose on the morning air.

"It's Edith!" Shirley exclaimed. "She doesn't know which way we turned."

"Edith!" I shouted.

The wailing stopped. We waited. A few moments later around the bend came Edith, her tail a furry flagpole.

We slowed our pace. Cats don't travel as fast as people, especially since they stop to investigate every new sound or smell and sit down to wash while they think about it.

We turned left on Oakcrest and waited.

Half our walking time was gone and we had covered only half a mile.

"I think we had better start back," said Phyllis.

"I'm sorry," I said. "Edith is holding us up too much. Maybe if we carried her, we could go faster."

Edith weighed twelve pounds at the time. If you have ever carried a ten-pound bag of sugar around to see how it feels to be ten pounds overweight, you know twelve pounds of cat can be a millstone.

What is more, Edith didn't want to be carried and kept squirming. We all took turns carrying her.

When we arrived on familiar grounds, I put Edith down. She dashed up a terrace and continued walking with us but far out of reach. No hikers were going to carry her again!

When I turned in at our house and opened the garage door, she flopped down on a strip of carpet and stayed there the rest of the morning.

Since then, when Edith is out and she sees us starting on our walk, she follows us a little way and then goes back home. So far I have never seen Edith make the same mistake twice.

I mentioned before Edith's fascination with water. Since kittenhood she has never lost her devotion to the study of the gushing garden hose, the dripping downspout, the cascading faucet, and the swirling sink drain.

One morning by accident I left the kitchen faucet running. When I came back into the kitchen a few minutes later, there stood Edith on the sink ledge, her neck outstretched to its limit, her tongue flicking in and out lapping up the water. She took 156 laps before she sat back, ran her tongue over her upper lip, and looked at me as if to say it was just what she liked.

Next morning when I opened the cupboard door where I keep the pills, she hopped up on the sink, ready for her drink.

"Edith," I told her, "you have a special porcelain bowl with your name on the side, which is filled every morning with fresh drinking water. Why don't you use it? Drinking out of the faucet wastes too much water. Have you any idea how much water costs, to say nothing of the sewer rent?"

Still she sat, smiling.

A two-quart watering can for the potted plants sat by the sink. I filled it and poured. She took 182 sips before the can was empty. She waited for me to refill it and took forty-five more.

Usually she comes for a drink whenever she hears the pill cupboard open. If I am outdoors and turn on the hose to fill a sprinkling can or to water a plant, she comes running. One day in the rain I saw her standing on a stone wall lapping water as it gushed from the downspout.

"Always keep a bowl of fresh drinking water available," say all the cat books.

A bowl of fresh water is the last place in the house from which cats will drink unless they can't find any other source.

Elmer Davis says in *Oh Being Kept by a Cat* that his cat likes to drink from the bathtub.

"If somebody runs a little for him," he writes, "he

drinks as much as he wants to and then pulls out the plug. That may be the accidental result of an impulse to play with a shiny chain, but it seems plausible that he has seen other people pull the plug when they are through with water in the bathtub and knows what will happen when he pulls it."

Generally cats like to drink flowing water better than the still variety. I heard of a cat that stirs the water in her bowl until it ripples and then drinks.

The plumber told me that after he installed a new toilet in the home of a customer, she called him to come back because the toilet kept flushing automatically.

"Eight or ten times a day when I am working in the kitchen, or sitting reading, I hear the new toilet flush. It's eerie, because there is nobody at home but me. If it keeps doing that all the time, our water bill will be tremendous."

The plumber checked the toilet but found nothing wrong.

He packed up his tools and was writing up his bill in the kitchen when both he and the housewife heard the toilet flush.

They rushed upstairs. Somebody was in the bathroom, all right. Crouching on the seat sat the family cat, watching the water swirl.

After the plumber put a different kind of handle on the toilet, the mysterious flushing ceased.

Just before Christmas one year Edith's special bowl slipped out of my hands and shattered. I replaced it with a Royal Doulton bowl with a border of rabbits running around the edge and a family of rabbits in the bottom of the bowl picking yellow apples from a tree. The mother rabbit and three of the babies have on pink jackets, and two boy rabbits wear blue. One of the boys is helping with the apples but the other lies stretched out under the tree with his front paws folded over his chest.

So far as I know, Edith has never taken one sip out of her bowl.

I have two bonsai plants that ought to be watered two times a day at least, but life is so complex that I often forget them and sometimes find one or the other keeled over in a faint.

I devised a kind of self-watering contraption. I placed between the two plants a blue pottery bowl that holds two quarts of water. I buried two strands of shoelace in the soil of each plant and dangled the other ends of the laces in the bowl. Capillary attraction sends the water up the laces and into the soil.

I was amazed at how the water level in the bowl went down. Those two plants drink almost two quarts of water a day.

One Sunday morning when I was sitting on the living room floor reading the newspaper, I heard the soft sound of water lapping. I thought perhaps something had sprung a leak, but all was quiet in the kitchen and bathrooms.

I went back to the paper. The lapping continued.

They mystery of the thirsty bonsai plants was solved.

Why does Edith prefer to drink day-old potted plant water out of a lime-encrusted pottery bowl when she has her own Bunnikins dish of nice, fresh water?

An acquaintance tells me that her cat can't see the water clearly in the bowl and doesn't like to get her nose wet. They solved the problem by letting a piece of cork float in the water. Another says that his cats will not drink out of small bowls but lap happily out of their fourteen-inch bowl.

One thing is certain. Every cat is different. It's up to us to find what our cats like; it's a sure thing it will never work the other way.

Edith's third W is washing. Besides keeping clean, cats have many reasons for washing.

Jennie, in Paul Gallico's book of the same name, gave a lecture on why cats wash:

"If you have committed any kind of error and anyone scolds you — wash. If you slip and fall off something and somebody laughs at you — wash.

"If you are getting the worst of an argument and want to break off hostilities until you have composed yourself, start washing...

"Whatever the situation, whatever difficulty you may be in you can't go wrong if you wash. If you come into a room full of people you do not know, sit right down in the midst of them and start washing. They'll end up by quieting down and watching you. Some noise frightens you into a jump — begin washing immediately.

"If somebody calls you and you don't care to come and still you don't wish to make it a direct insult — wash. If you've started to go off somewhere and can't remember where it was you wanted to go, sit right down and begin brushing up a little. It will come back to you. Something hurt you? Wash it.

"Tired of playing with someone who has been kind enough to take time and trouble and you want to break off without hurting his or her feelings? Start washing.

"Oh, there are dozens of things! Door closed and you're burning up because no one will open it for you — have yourself a little wash and forget it.

"Somebody petting another cat or dog in the same room, and you are annoyed over *that* — be nonchalant and wash. Feel sad — wash away your blues. Been picked up by someone you don't particularly fancy and who didn't smell good, wash him off immediately and pointedly where he can see you do it. Overcome by emotion — a wash will help you get a good grip on yourself again. Any time, anyhow, in any manner, for whatever purpose, wherever you are, whenever and why ever that you want to clear the air, or get a moment's respite or think things over — WASH!"

I have seen Edith wash for all Jennie's reasons.

One time I saw her leap for the bureau top, but she misjudged the distance and landed on the floor. She immediately began washing as if that was what she planned to do all the time.

I was planting bulbs one afternoon, and Edith was hanging around, jumping into every hole I dug. I put down the trowel and went down the steps to the garage to get a trash bag.

When I started around the corner and up the steps, I ran spang into Edith coming down them. She sat right down on a step and began washing. I know as well as I know my name that she was embarrassed because I had caught her following me.

One evening I saw her across the street in Moonbeam's yard. I called to her to come home. She turned, looked my way, sat down to wash a few licks, and then, as fast as a portly cat can, started to come across the street and up the hill through the ivy.

I stood holding the door open. As soon as she reached the top of the hill, she sat down on the grass and began washing. I became tired of waiting and closed the door. When she heard the door click, she stopped in mid-lick, hopped up on the windowsill and let me know she was ready to come in.

Insulated

A cat will walk through any open doorway or hop into any drawer, cupboard, or closet. Edith once spent a morning in the broom closet because I didn't see her go inside. She spent another morning in the linen closet.

She looks inside every grocery bag, every trash bag, every paper sack from the drug store, and every box delivered by the United Parcel Service.

Just before Edith's first Christmas in our house, I opened the attic door, planning to bring down the decorations. At the time, Edith was asleep on the filing cabinet in the office. As I reached to pull the cord that turns on the attic lights, I saw the periscope of her tail sailing up the attic steps.

"No! No! Edith! Not for cats!" I shouted, hurrying up the stairs after her. "Come back!"

Only a small part of the attic is floored; the rest is

covered with a deep layer of powdery, blown-in insulation. Over the bathrooms it is at least two feet deep, and so far as I know there is nothing to keep a cat from slipping down between the inner and outer walls.

If she fell down between the walls, she could suffocate. How could I get her out before something horrible happened?

I fetched the Bonkers box from the kitchen. Edith loves Bonkers and when she is outdoors, if I shake the box and call her, she will come running from as far away as the eighteenth tee at Community Golf Club.

I stood at the attic steps and called, rattling the Bonkers box.

Either Edith had found something more interesting to her or she had already sunk inextricably into the insulation.

In the attic the glare of the two light bulbs dangling on wires made seeing beyond them impossible.

"I'll get a flashlight," I called.

Panic began growing inside me. I couldn't remember where I kept the flashlight. I opened one drawer after another even though I knew the flashlight was too big to fit inside them.

"Now look here," I said to myself, "keep calm. Where did you last use the flashlight? It's probably still there."

So far as I could remember, I hadn't used the flashlight since the Dayton flood, and my house wasn't even built then.

Then joy swept through me. I always keep one flashlight by the fuse box.

Sure enough, the flashlight was there. I cleaned the dust off it and flicked the switch.

It did not light.

"Batteries," I said. "Where do I keep the batteries?"

I couldn't find the batteries.

I did know where my camera was and with shaking fingers took two batteries out of it.

I slid the batteries into the flashlight positive end up, negative end up, and positive and negative ends alternating.

The flashlight refused to flicker.

"I'm going to the store to get a new flashlight," I called up to Edith. "I'll be right back."

I grabbed my purse and the car keys and ran down to the garage.

Over hill and dale I sped, all the while imagining Edith suffocating in the horrible insulation. What is worse, I began thinking about an incident I had read not long before. A cat disappeared in a house, and the owners searched high and low for days. They went up to the attic many times and called the cat, but there was no answer.

A year after the cat disappeared, one of the owners found a loose board in the attic floor. He thrust his hand under the board and when he drew it out, the entire skin of his cat came away in his hand. They always wondered why the cat hadn't answered when they called.

"Your cat's lost in the insulation?" the hardware store clerk echoed when I told her the news. "Reminds me of our cat. He was missing for two days once and we could hear him crying in the walls. He had crawled through an opening in a closet and disappeared behind the plumbing."

"What — what happened to him?"

"Oh, we put a plate of food on the closet floor and after a while he came out."

I drove home faster than the speed limit allowed and took the steps to the first floor two at a time. With shaking fingers I pried open the plastic bubble that clamped the flashlight to its cardboard container, flicked on the light and bolted for the attic door.

There on the bottom step sat Edith with bits of insulation on her whiskers.

"Ow," she said and bounded off to her food dish.

Edith disappeared again one summer day.

Her luncheon dish remained untouched.

She did not come for her supper.

It was beginning to get dark when Catharine in response to a doleful call for help and carrying a flashlight, walked up the front steps. I was sitting on the porch.

"Have you called her?" she asked.

"About ten thousand times."

"The trouble is if she answered you, you wouldn't hear her. Edith!"

We both waited.

"I hear her!" she exclaimed. "She's right around here somewhere." She handed me the flashlight. "Her voice seems to be coming from over our heads," she continued, walking along the front of the house. "Shine the flashlight on the roof."

Edith meowed.

"She's up high somewhere."

Catharine called again and cocked her head.

"She answers every time I call. Don't you hear her?"

"No."

"Shine the flashlight here," Catharine said from the corner of the house.

An overhang about two feet wide runs around the edge of the roof. At the corners are gratings. I flashed the light over the grating and saw a movement.

"There she is!"

A beige paw hung wiggling through the grating. We could see Edith's face behind the louvers.

"How did she ever get in there? How will we ever get her out?"

"I think she crawled in there from the attic," said Catharine.

We dashed for the attic stairs and turned on the light. Waves of heat rolled over us. Edith came lunging through the insulation and jumped into Catharine's arms.

Once back on the main floor, she dashed for her food dish.

When the bowl was empty, she washed her face, her chest, her back, her stomach, her tail. Then she leaped into my lap, turned around, settled down, and went to sleep.

"How did she get up in the attic?" Catharine asked. "It must have been absolutely scorching up there."

"Dorothy was here cleaning today. She opened the attic door sometime because when I came home this afternoon, the attic exhaust fan was on. She evidently didn't see Edith go up the stairs. I recall now that when I came home, Dorothy said she hadn't seen her all day."

Thanks heavens Catharine has good ears. I might not have opened the attic door for days.

Being mewed up in the hot attic has not lessened its

attractiveness to Edith. She has learned the special sound the attic door makes when it is opened, and if she is in the house, she makes a dash for the doorway. I have learned, however, that if I leave the door open, she will come back down into the house, when the pleasures of the biggest litter box on our street pall.

New Life and a Death

Until Edith moved into our house I had no idea we had so many cats in the neighborhood. Moonbeam, Edith's first visitor, continued to come twice a day and wore a path down the hill through the ivy.

Other cats occasionally strolled through the yard. If Edith was in the house, she watched them through her window, switching her tail from side to side, and growling. If she was outside, the cats growled at each other and stared almost nose to nose until the interloper gave up and disappeared down the hill.

One morning when I opened the door for Edith to go out, she froze on the threshold. All cats hesitate before going through an open door, looking for an eagle swooping down from above and sniffing the air for a passing dog or bear. This time, however, Edith stared at a spot on the porch and refused to move.

On the porch staring back crouched an orange-and-white cat.

When she saw me holding the door, she began a long tale. I thought she was asking me please, please would I take pity on a poor, hungry cat and give her something to eat and drink.

I had a bag of dry cat food that Edith didn't like. I filled a bowl and another of water and set them on the porch.

The orange cat sniffed at the food, sat down, curled her tail around her toes and began to eat. When the bowl was empty, she begged for a second and emptied the bowl of water. She finished off the second bowl of food, gave herself a good washing, and stretched out on the porch carpet for a nap.

Meanwhile Edith slipped out the doorway behind her and disappeared.

Several hours later I opened the door to see if Edith had come back for lunch. At the sound of the doorlatch Orange Cat ran from a spot under a taxus and began to cry, longing in her eyes.

I looked out into the yard. Peeking from around the oak tree was Edith, her gaze on the cat.

"Come on in, Edith," I called. "Time for lunch."

Edith took a step forward and crouched. I opened the door. Orange Cat tried to come in.

"Not you," I said, fending her off with my foot. "This is Edith's house."

Orange Cat sat down and looked hopeful.

I walked out and picked Edith up. As we passed Orange Cat, Edith growled.

Later I sat on one of the iron chairs on the porch. Orange Cat approached, timidly at first, ready to run at the slightest movement of my hand or foot. After a long time she put a feathery paw on my knee, looked into my eyes and told me all about her troubles.

Somehow she had strayed from her home or, perhaps, had been tossed out. Her long coat was matted and full of burrs.

I hoped she would go away, but she didn't. In two days she had figured out the routine of our household and fitted herself into it as much as I would let her. She learned the sound of my car and came running the minute I turned into the driveway. When I went away, she sat on the porch and watched, her posture indicating she would guard the house until my return. Whenever I returned, she was sitting there waiting.

The nights grew cold. In the mornings when Edith hopped up on my bed and stretched out her whole length on the electric blanket, I lay awake thinking about Orange Cat huddled outdoors somewhere in the cold.

In the afternoon she took naps outdoors under the picture window and when she woke, walked along the ledge, looking in and opening her mouth in a silent meow. When I sat at the kitchen table having breakfast or reading, her ears appeared above the sill and then her round, dark eyes and then her mouth. She mewed and mewed to come in and warm herself by the fire.

Her plight devastated me. I hadn't the heart not to feed her, but I couldn't let her in.

One of my colleagues at the paper was Larry Newman, a fellow cat lover. I made a plea for him to take her.

He couldn't upset the equanimity of his own cat, who was very old, by introducing a new cat into the household. He suggested that I should write a column about Orange Cat's dilemma. Jim Zofkie, the reader's representative, arranged for two technicians to set up a tape recorder and hook it into the telephone. I gave the telephone number in the column and asked readers who would be willing to take her to call.

The column appeared on a Saturday morning. On Monday when I checked the tape, I found fifty calls. One young woman who had lost a cat eight years before hoped that Orange Cat was hers. Another whose pure-bred Persian's disappearance had broken her heart called.

"I'd just love to take your cat," said another woman. "When I was a little girl, I brought home every kitten I could find, but my mother would never let me have one. She told me that when I grew up and married and had my own home, then I could have all the cats I wanted to. Now I am grown up and married, but wouldn't you know — I married a man who is allergic to cats."

Six people who had cats to give away left their names and numbers.

One woman volunteered to take Orange Cat. She even came to pick her up.

After she was gone, I called the people who had cats to give away and gave them the numbers of others who had indicated they might take Orange Cat.

On Wednesday the woman who had taken her brought her back.

My heart sank. I had the cat back and all my prospects were gone. I went to work on Thursday with glum spirits.

In the mail was a letter from Anne Kirchner.

"My home is, I think, eminently suitable for Orange Cat," she wrote. "I have a fenced back yard with a lilac tree for snoozing under. Plenty of food is available and three litter boxes are conveniently placed. A padded chair is provided by the window for bird watching.

There are balls to chase, grocery bags to crawl into, and cartons to sit in.

"Two other friendly cats will provide companionship. My husband Rudolph and I have comfortable laps for sitting."

With lyric spirits I put Orange Cat into Edith's traveling case and set off in the car to drive across town.

The Kirchners live on a lovely, shaded street. They both welcomed me at the door when I carried the case into their living room.

I opened the door and Orange Cat emerged.

She was not the bouncy cat who had been living on my front porch. Her tail, which had been a golden plume held high at my house, now dragged on the floor. She drooped. She had no brisk confidence. She looked like a tattered refugee.

She crept along the wall and disappeared under a sofa.

When I left, I worried the Kirchners might be disappointed in her. She wasn't really a pretty cat. All the rest of the week I became a little panicky whenever the telephone rang.

Two weeks later I received a letter from Anne. "She spent the rest of the day under the sofa," Anne said. "After supper I hauled her out and told her not to be silly. She had a dish of milk with the chill taken off, and when I sat on the sofa to read, I patted the cushion and she jumped up. One paw followed another until she was finally cozy in my lap. My, she is heavy.

"She spent the first week in the garage. I leave the door open about a foot so the cats can go out and come in. One night she skipped out about suppertime and set off down the sidewalk. I made the mistake of giving chase. Down the sewer she went. I was afraid to leave to get a flashlight and got down on my hands and knees with my head in the sewer calling, 'Kitty, kitty, kitty.'

"A nice neighbor jogging by sent his daughter for a flashlight. I heard rustling in what I thought was water and feared she would drown.

"With the light we saw nothing but leaves and a big pipe. The young man said he was familiar with the neighborhood cats and not to worry. They have a bridge table and candle down there and play cards.

"I went home and left the side door open. A couple of hours later there she was with her face pressed against the patio door. Now when she comes home late Rudolph says she must have a good hand."

Anne named her Felix, because it means happy.

Every Christmas Felix sends a card to Edith, and Edith sends one to Felix.

After Orange Cat left, I stopped leaving food on the front porch. For some time Moonbeam's visits had become infrequent. Whenever Edith was outdoors and Moonbeam did come over for a little snack, I could count on her letting me know he was there.

Finally Moonbeam's visits stopped.

One day I saw Mary Haffner, his owner, at the mailbox and asked about him.

Her usually merry face grew long.

"He was sick for a long time," she said. "I took him to Dr. Coatney, who did what he could for him. But finally when he became unable to walk, Dr. Coatney said the best thing for Moonbeam was to have him put down."

Mary rubbed her hand across her eyes.

"We had him for eighteen years," she said. "Afterwards I had a nice note from Dr. Coatney. He said he felt very bad about Moonbeam and he would always remember him as a very fine patient."

That evening I told Edith about Moonbeam, but she made no comment.

The next day Mary reported that she saw Edith sitting on her windowsill. She had never seen her there before.

I think she was looking for Moonbeam.

It has been several years now since Moonbeam died. The path his little paws wore through the ivy up our hill has become overgrown. Edith still goes to Moonbeam's house on her rounds, but now she goes the long way around, down our front steps, up the hilly street and up his driveway.

He was a lovely cat.

Kidnapped

One afternoon a day or so after Christmas Edith hopped up on my desk and sat down on my papers.

I keep a desk chair right by my own for her. After she has conducted an inventory of the desk top, rubbing her chin against the pencil holder, pushing a few paper clips around, and sniffing for rubber bands, she usually curls up on the desk seat, turns up her chin, and drifts off to sleep.

Occasionally I rub my hand over her soft fur. It amazes me how trusting she is. She never stirs under the touch of my fingers.

This time she slept for an hour, lifted her head, stretched, and jumped to the floor. In a moment I heard her name tag clicking against her food dish in the kitchen. Then she appeared at my side, in her eyes a question.

"All right, Edith." I rose and followed her to the front door. She paused on the threshold and then stepped out into the cold. "Don't stay out too long."

By dinner time dark had settled over our hill. I opened the door, expecting Edith to dash in as she had every time before.

But no Edith waited on the porch.

I prepared dinner and ate at the table by the window, but she did not hop up on the sill. I watched the evening news and every time a commercial came on hurried to the door. The hand on the thermometer crept down as the evening wore on. By midnight the temperature was zero, and still Edith had not returned.

I could not sleep. Every hour on the hour I padded out through the kitchen and opened the front door, hoping to see her curled up under the wrought iron chair. She was never there.

She was not on the porch in the morning. I knew her well enough to know that if she could come home, she would have. I could envision her poor body lying in a street, crushed by a car. Perhaps she had wandered into somebody's garage and was locked inside. Allie, a cat who lives across the street, was missing for two weeks once. She had wandered into a neighbor's garage and was there when the door closed. They drove off to Florida and were gone a fortnight.

I felt a cold hand close around my heart. I made a list of all the things I could do to try to find her.

I called the newspaper and put an ad in the Lost and Found.

SICSA has a registration service, and Edith's picture and description is on record there. I called, but a recorded voice said the adoption center was closed until after New Year and for help to call the Humane Society.

"I want to report that my cat is missing," I said to the woman at the Humane Society who answered. I gave her my name.

There was a pause.

"You don't mean *Edith*?"

"Yes, Edith."

"Good heavens, we read about her in the paper all the time. Tell me what she looks like and I'll go see whether we have a cat here that answers her description."

"Edith is a brown-and-orange tabby with fawn-colored toes on the outside of her paws."

When she came back, she said no, Edith had not been brought in but she would post a note so the staff members would be on the lookout for her. She also suggested calling the Kettering Street Department.

I called.

"You don't mean *Edith*?" the woman who answered asked. "Oh, dear."

It was comforting to know that people at the street department had read about Edith's adventures and cared about her.

"I'll get word to the drivers," she added. "If we pick her up, I'll call you."

I called the Oakwood police. Oakwood is not far from our home, and Edith had hiked through it when she ran away from the Booker house.

"We do have a report of a cat found on Wisteria Drive," said the woman who answered. "Is Edith a gray tabby?"

I called the Hedricks next door and the Haffners across the street because Edith sometimes walks into their garages. They looked, but Edith was not to be found. Willa Hedrick searched under every bush in her woods.

I called Catharine. She and her daughter, Mary Ames, came at once to help in the search. We scoured the neighborhood for blocks around, calling, and looking into garage windows.

Catharine drove up to the house on Wisteria on the off chance that the gray cat might be Edith. When she returned, she said it was not Edith but she was a very nice cat, and the woman who found her said I might have her if Edith didn't come back.

I didn't want any other cat; I wanted Edith. After

Catharine went home, I washed up Edith's drinking bowl and her food dish and stood looking at them. "Edith!" I wailed. "Edith, where are you? Come back. Come back. Edith!" Really, on the stage it would have been a harrowing scene.

I paced around the house wondering what more I could do to find her. I printed a few notices to put on telegraph poles.

I am not a person who ever asks others to do a favor for me unless I am in the direst of straits. This was ever direr than direst. I called up Bill Wild. At the time he was editor of the editorial page of the newspaper for which I wrote.

I poured out my grief to him.

"Do you think you could put a little notice about Edith on the op-ed page and maybe run her picture with it?" I asked. "She has a picture on file in the reference library.

He said he would consider it.

The day dragged on. Edith did not return and nobody called. I kept the vigil all night, hurrying to the door every hour, creeping back to my damp pillow, and crying some more.

When the paper came the next morning, Edith still had not returned. Hopefully I turned to the op-ed page. Nothing. Well, after all, it was pretty nervy of me to ask.

Then I looked at the editorial page. There was Edith's picture over this editorial:

Feline fame aside, where's Edith?

Edith is making the news again by disappearing from Roz Young's northwest Kettering home. Little ingrate.

The search has disclosed so far that Edith is as well or better known than Roz is, to the police and street department personnel, at any rate. The columnist thought she was out of the cat business after a recent well-reported adoption effort, but Edith must have thought it was exciting and things were getting dull.

Edith, wherever you are, please call 293-9722 or 225-2380 today, and be ready for a good talking to.

I sat there at the breakfast table reading the editorial over and over and looking at Edith's picture and thinking what a wonderful man Bill Wild is. I cried some more.

The telephone rang. I jumped.

"You don't know me," a man's voice said, "but I was reading the paper over breakfast, and I have your cat. If you will tell me where you live, I will bring her to you."

I used to think Wordsworth had strange anatomy because his heart leaped when he beheld a rainbow in the sky.

I was wrong. Hearts do leap sometimes. Mine did then.

I gave him the directions and ran to get dressed. Then I watched the driveway until a black car appeared.

A tall man in a brown parka hurried up the steps. He had Edith in his arms. He held her out and I took her in my arms.

"Please come in," I said.

"No, I'm on my way to work."

"But how did you find Edith?"

He told me what had happened at his house, but when I asked his name, he shook his head.

"I'm so embarrassed I won't even tell you," he said and down the steps he went.

When I shut the door, the sun came out even though it was still dark. Joy raced through the whole household. I hugged Edith and capered around the kitchen as if I were a springtime lamb.

I set out a big bowl of food for her.

I canceled the ad in the paper and called my neighbors, Catharine, the Humane Society, the street department, Bill Wild, and the police. O frabjous day.

Two mornings later on New Year's Day Edith was on the editorial page again.

Happy 1986! It's the Cat's Meow

Truth is stranger than fiction, as Lord Byron wrote. We'll get to that in a minute.

The first truth is that there was some skepticism on the editorial board about the wisdom of running the snippet on Roz Young's lost cat, Edith, Tuesday morning. It was fortunate — and absurdly good luck — that the wisdom of heart prevailed over the logic of head.

A reader saw the editorial note and Edith's picture. His small daughter had recently brought in a stray cat, said to be collarless. A little detective work turned up Edith's collar in the little girl's bureau drawer, and a bit of a catnapping tale. He called Roz. Now cat, collar, and owner are happily reunited.

Count on Roz writing about it in a week or so. But she didn't get the name of her benefactor or the now catless child. Some veteran reporter she is.

Anyway, it's a nice way to start off 1986. You couldn't make up a beginning any better

than that, unless you had the name of some-
one who, oh, so badly, wants a cat and could
be matched with another half dozen cats,
none named Edith, that turned up in Roz's
quest.

Thank goodness the little girl's father was the kind of person who read the editorials. Otherwise I might not ever have seen Edith again.

Edith Bites a Friend and Gets a Surname

When I was a junior in high school, we read a poem by Alfred Noyes, who issued a kind of invitation:

> Come down to Kew in lilac time
> (it isn't far from London)
> And you will wander hand in hand with
> love in nature's wonderland.

I didn't even know what Kew was in those days, but it sounded like somewhere I would like to go. It would be all right with me to wander hand in hand with love, and I greatly admired the smell of old-fashioned lilacs that bloomed in our back dooryard.

Edith was about three when I signed up to take a garden tour of England, which included a day trip to

Kew Gardens. I really didn't expect to wander hand in hand with anybody, but the lilacs would be blooming.

One morning ten days before the plane was to leave, Edith did not get up when I did. Usually she is on the counter with her nose in the dish before I have finished unscrewing the lid to the glass jar where I keep her food. This morning she did not stir out of bed when I filled her dish, or opened the door to get the newspaper.

I knew Edith well enough by then that if food didn't interest her, she must be sick. By 9:30 she was in her carrying case on the way to Dr. Coatney's office.

She said nary a word during the drive. But the second I opened the door to the clinic, she lifted her voice in despair. I tried to get her to be quiet like the other cats in the waiting room, but she wailed unendingly.

She stopped crying when Dr. Coatney examined her eyes, ears, throat, and chest.

When he took her temperature, she yelled, and she yelled louder when he felt her kidneys.

"She has picked up an infection," he said. "We'll have to give her a couple of shots."

I held her for the shots. At the first one she hid her head in the crook of my arm and cried.

"Now this one will really hurt," he said and stuck in the needle.

Edith screeched and buried an eye tooth in my wrist. I was dumbfounded. Sweet little, mild little Edith had never so much as scratched me before.

Dr. Coatney put some antibiotic cream on the puncture, gave me a bottle of twice-a-day medicine for Edith and sent us home.

Next morning my arm was red, hot to the touch and so painful I could not use it.

I went to Lewis, my physician and Catharine's husband. He said I had a Pasteurella infection. Long ago Louis Pasteur identified several rod-shaped bacteria sometimes carried by cats and dogs, and the bacteria can be pathogenic to human beings.

I went home with pills and a regimen of cold compresses.

I developed a sympathy for persons with only one arm. To wash oneself, to comb hair, fasten hooks, pull on stockings, open envelopes, tie shoe laces, cook, and spread butter on bread with only one hand, all require ingenuity. For four days I couldn't even write my name.

Edith was a gem through all my troubles. Every morning and night when I took her bottle of antibiotic out of the refrigerator and showed it to her, she hopped up on the table, tipped back her head, and drank the dose from the dropper. I didn't even have to hold her.

One morning I couldn't find the dropper. I poured a little medicine into a teaspoon.

"Drink this, Edith."

She drank it.

Edith recovered her bounce in two days, but I didn't. Five days before the trip, Lewis said he thought I might not be able to go. I had not taken out cancellation insurance and the thought of losing all that money, as well as missing the lilacs at Kew, depressed me.

The day before the trip he said I could go but I would have to take an antibiotic for two weeks of the trip.

I went on the trip, but the medicine made me sleepy, so I missed most of the scenery between gardens.

I was so groggy by the time we arrived at Kew, I sat down on a bench and took a nap and missed the lilacs.

I hadn't been back from England more than a week when I noticed in the church bulletin that we were getting new hymnals, and that anyone who wished to dedicate a hymnal to a family member could do so by dropping a check for ten dollars into the collection plate.

A bookplate giving the name of the person for whom the hymnal was dedicated and the name of the donor would be placed in the inside cover of the book. Hymnals could be dedicated in memoriam to the dead or in thanksgiving for the living.

Before Edith came, when somebody asked me whether I ever became lonely living by myself, I said no, but it wasn't the truth. Holidays with no family can get to be lonely times. I had a friend once who went to the railroad station every Christmas morning and took the first train, no matter where it was going. She rode all day, got off and stayed in a hotel, and rode back the next day.

After Edith came, I had no more lonely times. She was always with me, wanting breakfast, needing a brushing, asking to go out, to come in, to go out, to come in, begging for breakfast, lunch, afternoon snack, dinner, bedtime snack. If I took a nap, she took a nap. If I dug a hole for plants in the garden, she dug my holes bigger.

I decided to dedicate a hymnal in thanksgiving for Edith.

She would need a surname for her bookplate. Years ago I married a man named Young and naturally became a Young, too. But inside me I always felt like a McPherson, the name with which I was born. I gave Edith my maiden name, wrote out the check, and dropped it into the offering plate one Sunday morning.

I did not mention that Edith McPherson was a cat. Some members in our church might regard with elevated eyebrows a hymnal dedicated to a cat.

The church bulletin one week said that the new hymnals had arrived, and the next Sunday they would be distributed.

When we arrived, the hymnals were all stacked by the altar. The rector announced that we would sing "Come, my soul, thou must be waking" out of the old hymnal. Then we were to walk by rows to the front of the church, hand the old hymnal to an usher in exchange for the new one, and go back to the pew still singing. We would send the old hymnals to a church in Africa that didn't have any.

The exchange worked out very well. I did not get the hymnal with Edith's name in it, so I waited until after church and walked around looking in the hymnals until I found it. I planned to put it in the rack in front of my regular seat.

Alas. Whoever had lettered the bookplate made a mistake. The plate read:

> *This Hymnal 1982 is presented to*
> *Christ Episcopal Church*
> *in memoriam for*
> *Edith McPherson*
> *by Rosamond Young*

I sang out of the hymnal for a few Sundays, but every time I looked at that "in memoriam" I felt upset.

Finally one Saturday morning I put a little note in my column telling about Edith's bookplate in the new hymnal.

"My cat Edith is only three years old," I wrote. "Cats can live to be eighteen or even twenty. Edith could well outlive me. I am unhappy having to sing every Sunday out of a hymnal that is dedicated to the memory of Edith when she is still alive and well."

The next day was Sunday. Wilson Austin stopped by my seat. His face was pink.

"I'm the one who made the mistake," he said. "I thought Edith McPherson was your mother."

"Oh, no," I replied. "Her name was Isabel."

"I'll make a new bookplate," he said.

He did, and all is well now in my pew.

Celebrity Cat

A cat whose picture and the story of whose kidnapping has appeared on the editorial page of a newspaper that goes into two hundred thousand homes in our part of the world gains a certain amount of fame.

Time was when I walked down the street or went to the grocery store, people stopped to chat about the weather or the election or whatever.

It has been a long time since anybody asked me how I am. What my friends and even strangers want to know is how is Edith.

One day when I stopped for lunch in Lebanon, which is halfway between Dayton and Cincinnati, a woman walked past the table. Then she walked past again, going the other way, and stopped.

"Pardon me," she said, "but do you have a cat named Edith?"

One night at a restaurant in Waynesville as I walked to my table, I heard a woman say to her husband, "There goes Edith's mother."

Once I was invited to give a speech at the local literacy society. I had a serious speech ready, and after the chairman introduced me, I opened my mouth to begin. A woman in the audience waved her hand and shouted, "What we want to know is how is Edith?"

At holidays Edith gets cards from cats she doesn't even know, and often their owners write to tell her about some little adventure or send her their pictures. Her is a letter she received one Christmas from Mrs. Raymond Nagel:

Dear Edith:

At our house we have a spunky little cat who looks just like you. Her name is Nadine.

We found Nadine stuck in our front door one spring day about three years ago. Somewhere she had acquired some eccentric habits that endeared her to us. She would not eat from a dish until the contents were tipped out onto the floor. Anything that dribbled, gurgled, or rustled was endless fascination to her.

Nadine was crippled; a youthful trauma, the doctor said. She had had a dislocated hip, which had never been treated. And so she developed her own peculiar hobbling gait. We took her to our veterinarian, who found that she was pregnant with one kitten. We were delighted and marked the calendar with a big red X. Two weeks later Nadine wandered away from home and when she returned, we could tell she was ill.

The vet said she had suffered a blow to the abdomen, and the kitten was dead. The surgery he performed was massive, and she remained in intensive care for a week. When we finally were allowed to pick her up, the vet said he had inadvertently nicked a femoral artery on her good leg and there was nerve damage.

She now dragged her other leg on the opposite side.

In six weeks Nadine had compensated for that, too, using her tail as a rudder, she could jump fences and chase butterflies in our vegetable garden.

Nadine prospered and grew sleek and fat. Nearly everything she saw was edible, including cold cream, guest soaps, and toothpaste. Reprimands became out of the question; every time we shook a newspaper at her, her limp became more profound. She became adept at the game of ambush. This consisted of a perfectly timed leap at anyone coming down the stairs. In just five seconds she could shred a pair of hose and disappear behind a vase on the landing.

She became the terror of the household and an unmerciful bully to our other two cats.

Last Friday my husband and I were loading our car for a Christmas party when Nadine ran out of the house to investigate what we were doing. A hit-and-run driver struck her.

Yet another time we raced to the hospital with Nadine, and the outlook was grim. After half a day's wait, we learned that she had a skull fracture, a broken jaw, and a concussion. She had lost her teeth on one side. We spent an agonizing night at home while her life hung in the balance. Today we learned that she staggered to her feet and sniffed at her food. She is disoriented and her eyes may never be right, but when her jaw is wired and her teeth are pulled, we can bring her home for the holidays. Nadine's life is our gift to each other for the Yuletide.

I wanted to share her story with you. I know you would approve of her and appreciate her courage.

Merry Christmas, Edith.

Two years later as Edith's amanuensis I wrote to inquire about Nadine and received a prompt reply:

Dearest Edith:

How kind of you to remember me. It's always nice to have a pen pal, especially now that I have just become a shut-in due to approaching cold weather. Oh, yes, my _dear, my troubles and surgeries seem endless, but I cope, I cope._

When we last chatted I had just been run over. That was a week before Christmas and it caused my people a great deal of anguish. I had to stay in intensive care for ten days, but gradually I was allowed home visits until I could get around on my own. Alas, my friend, I have lost my sight. It's not a total loss, thank goodness; I have some vision in one eye. I have always considered myself fortunate in that I have a survivor's personality although sometimes I am sorely tried. My people had to have all my teeth removed also — as a result of my broken jaw's not healing properly. My physician seems to think a humidifier will allay my asthma attacks, and we hope to have one installed soon.

I came out to visit you when you made that personal appearance at Books & Company, but had an attack of shyness at the last minute — so many people!

To add to my personal situation, I am not an only cat — but rather from a three-cat family. There is Tess (of the D'urbervilles, a victim of her own provocative beauty) and a thoroughly crude ten-pound kitten named Bernie Kaspar, who is a sports buff and has no social graces (wears a Browns' collar, for heaven's sakes).

My people just bought a goose down comforter for their bed and I find it lovely for napping and sleeping, *too, if I can crawl under when they are asleep. The family doesn't seem to realize that cats are, after all, the best judges of comfort alive.*

My sense of smell and taste are gone forever because of my concussion, so it is necessary that I try eating a variety of things not usually considered as cat fare. Anything with noodles and gravy is acceptable, but bean sprouts are truly dreadful. I am a gourmand, however, and sample all offerings with good humor and a light heart.

You are well, I trust? How is your weight coming? My girth has gotten away from me (the hysterectomy, you know). My people despair of me. I take great pride in that I can still jump a four-foot chain link fence. There is a white squirrel in our neighborhood that really stands out in the squirrel community and this certainly distracts me to no end. I have always preferred white meat and mean to have him yet.

Please keep in touch. Keep well and safe.
Sincerely,
Nadine

Nadine spoke in her letter of having gone to see Edith at Books & Company.

Annye Camara, who with her husband, Joe Neri, owns the book shop, invited Edith to appear on behalf of SICSA.

For every book the store sold on the day of Edith's appearance Annye said she would give ten percent of the sale to SICSA, the adoption agency where I found Edith.

I thought it would be fun, and Edith made no objection when I told her about it.

She was to appear between seven and eight o'clock in the evening, and I planned to arrive fifteen minutes early.

I gave Edith's coat a good brushing and put her into the carrying case. Even though we were early, the parking lot at Town and Country was filled. Annye was waiting outside the store. She smiled.

"There are over one hundred people inside already," she said.

Annye had provided a dish of food, water, some toys, and a litter box. At first Edith didn't want to come out of her carrying case, but after some coaxing she ventured out.

The crowd was so great nobody could see her. Annye organized everybody into a line. Alice Lavery, head of SICSA, had come, and she volunteered to hold Edith on her lap. Edith rose to the occasion. She sat facing the line while everybody filed past her. They all wanted to pat her, and she didn't mind at all. In fact she gave a little "Ow" to each one.

Some of the visitors brought pictures of their cats to show Edith. She received some presents, too — toys, two bags of catnip, a pan of fudge, a plush bed, and an invitation to appear at the Kitty Hawk cat show.

The party lasted an hour. Everybody but Edith had refreshments. Edith was too excited to eat. By Annye's count three hundred people came to see her, and she raised $570 for SICSA.

Then Number 10 Wilmington Place, a retirement home, invited Edith to come to a Christmas open house. The dining room at Number 10 is open every Sunday for brunch, and Edith was to receive guests in the library in the afternoon. On the Thursday before the open house so many people had made reservations for brunch that the manager had to send out for extra tables. On Friday the reservations were closed.

Edith sat on the library sofa for about half an hour while four hundred folks crowded in to see her. After that she became tired and crawled behind some books and took a nap.

She received an invitation to attend a party at Bethany Lutheran Village.

Several years before Edith came to live in our house, I had put my name on the waiting list for Bethany. I did it because I don't have any family and thought I ought to make some arrangements to be looked after when I became really old or have some other disaster. I wasn't happy about the prospects of leaving my hilltop home with its flower garden and trees, but that was a long way off and maybe the day would never come.

I was pleased when Edith received the invitation; I wanted her to see where her new home would be at that far-off day when my name worked its way to the top of the list and I decided to move.

The party was in a large room ordinarily used for church services. Many residents came — some walking, some on canes, some in wheelchairs. Several speakers appeared on the program, but Edith was the one everybody wanted to see.

Men and women crowded around and stroked her soft fur. One woman in a wheelchair asked to hold her, and I put Edith on her lap. She put her arms around Edith and kissed her.

When Edith jumped out of the woman's arms, she smiled and I saw tears in her eyes.

"I had a cat before I came here," she said.

A feeling of unease rose in my mind, but I was too busy to think about it then.

She received an invitation to appear on *Collage*, a TV show produced by Paul Law.

Edith is not much of a TV fan, although she will watch a show for half an hour or so, particularly if there is lots of action. I was enthusiastic, though, dreaming that Edith would sit on my lap as she had on Alice's at Books & Company. The camera would zoom in on her beautiful face and love would break out all over the Miami Valley.

I brushed her coat until it gleamed. I told her how she was about to have her opportunity to join Morris and all those other cats on TV who advertise pet food. Some advertising man might see her and soon she would be a star with Edith T-shirts and Edith endorsements for Bonkers and goodness knows what else.

Paul said he would pick us up an hour before camera time so Edith would have time to put on her makeup. She traveled to the station in her case, but once there I let her out to explore the premises. She roamed the studio, stalking along the perimeter of the dark room, stepping over cables, stacks of boxes, ladders, around cameras and light stands.

Her normal voice is dulcet and ladylike. Not that night, it wasn't. From a dark corner rose piercing howls.

"Yeow!" Edith shouted, "Yeow!" I don't like this place, she was saying. I want to go home. She shouted right up to time for the program.

When the program began, I picked her up and set her on my lap.

At home Edith will not sit on anybody's lap unless it is her own idea. I tried to hold her on my lap as the camera and red lights came on. I held her by the scruff of her neck and blew into her face, a practice some books say will comfort a distraught cat.

Edith squirmed and twisted. Down onto the floor she leaped, yowling as she went.

She paced back and forth across the set, howling. All the viewers could see was the tip of her tail as it crossed the set.

Nobody had a chance to see how beautiful she is. Now there will never be any Edith T-shirts or endorsements.

Although Edith flunked her TV appearance, she still has a chance for one endorsement, I think.

"Imagine how your teeth would feel if you never brushed them," said the folder Dr. Coatney handed me when I took Edith in for her feline leukemia booster shot. "Well, the same applies to your pet's mouth. Unless you are regularly providing some form of dental care, you are neglecting an important feature in the overall health of your pet."

The folder explained that cats can get peridontal disease ranging from gingivitis, plaque, tartar, bad breath, serious bleeding, receded or eroded gums, and loose or infected teeth.

Dr. Coatney removed scales of tartar from Edith's teeth with the same kind of scraper my dentist uses on me.

I stood by the table appalled, watching poor Edith patiently letting him scour away at her teeth. By my neglect I had violated Edith's rights and subjected her to all kinds of harmful possibilities.

When we left the office, we took along a special toothbrush for cats and a tube of enzymatic dentifrice.

"Edith," I said next morning, "we are going to clean your teeth."

She jumped up on the table to inspect the brush and tube.

I know better than to sneak up on Edith with wash cloth, damp cotton ball, medicine dropper, comb, brush or any other object I intend to use on her without explaining how I am going to use it. After the explanation she usually thinks of an errand she had under the dresser, but I am bigger than she is.

This time I squeezed a bit of toothpaste onto the brush and sat on the floor with Edith clamped between my legs.

"For the first few cleanings," said the directions, "gently hold the mouth shut with one hand. Lift the lip on one side of the mouth and brush the outside surfaces of the teeth. Increase the number of teeth brushed each time until your pet accepts the brush willingly."

Edith did not accept the first session willingly. She tried to back away, but there was nowhere to back. Then she squirmed around and faced me, her eyes wide with apprehension.

"This is for your own good," I said, trying to speak calmly. "We want you to have beautiful teeth and no peridontal disease. Now open your mouth."

"Yow," said Edith and clamped it shut.

With persistence I was able to get a little of the dentifrice on a few teeth and a lot of it on her lips and muzzle.

She chomped her jaws a few times and settled down to lick the paste off her fur.

Directions for cleaning the insides of the teeth call for more hands than most of us have. "Place one hand over the muzzle, gently squeeze the lips on one side between the back teeth, which will keep the mouth open.

"At the same time with your other hand pull the head back firmly so that the mouth will stay open. Now with your other hand brush the inside of the teeth at the opposite side. Repeat the procedure with the other side.

"Good luck! Your pet will certainly appreciate your efforts."

Hah. Tell that to Edith.

She had her first brushing on Monday. On Wednesday when I took out the brush and toothpaste, she hopped up on the table and looked quizzically at me and at the brush. I squeezed some dentifrice on the brush and took Edith's head in my hand.

"Open your mouth," I said.

Mirabile dictu, she opened her mouth.

I cleaned her teeth all around without one bit of struggle. She likes the toothpaste. She even let me work a little on the insides of her mouth.

When we get our routine perfected, I think we may go on TV with a new kind of toothpaste ad.

Edith Eater

Dr. Coatney said that Edith should eat dry cat food. She has four or five kinds in glass jars for variety so it won't get stale. Sometimes she has little bits of my food. She likes the insides of lima beans, rice, noodles, tomato soup, corn, and asparagus.

Once I gave her an egg yolk. After that she came running every time she heard the egg beater whirring. Although she can see a squirrel across the street, she had to put her nose a quarter of an inch from the egg beater to see if it was running properly.

One day when I made a souffle for company, I had put her outdoors in order to get the eggs beaten in time. I had poured the mixture into the souffle dish when the doorbell rang, and Edith came in with the guests.

What with greetings and hanging up coats, it was five minutes before I could get back to the kitchen to put the souffle in the oven. On the counter by the dish sat Edith, licking her chops. Little tongue marks edged the dish. The guests never knew that the souffle meant for three that day had really served four.

I set six blue pansies in a globe-shaped porcelain vase on the table.

Edith came hurrying in to inspect the flowers. She poked her paw into the vase and upset it, scattering the pansies and spilling water on the cloth. She picked up a pansy by its stem and began to chew. As the stem shortened, the pansy neared her mouth. Finally nothing was left except the blossom. I took a picture of Edith with a pansy between her teeth. She reminded me of Carmen.

One day in a bookshop I picked up a copy of *The Natural Cat, a Holistic Guide for Finicky Owners*, by Anitra Frazier, a cat groomer in New York City.

In the book Anitra tells about sending love messages across the room and wrapping a hot water bottle in a sock you have worn and to put it in the carrying case when you have to take the cat to the vet on a winter day.

When I read the chapter on diet, I went into a decline.

According to the book the preservatives, coloring, and artificial flavoring used in many commercial cat foods are dangerous to cats. The high ash contents are a prime suspect in causing cystitis and bladder stones. The protein content is too low.

Anitra recommends special canned cat food that has no preservatives or harmful meat by-products. To this she suggests adding a vitamin-mineral mix of yeast powder, kelp, lecithin, wheat germ, bran, and dolomite. In addition a cat should have cod liver oil and Vitamin E three times a week and morsels of broiled chicken, some vegetables, and alfalfa sprouts.

I made a list and took it to a health food store. The saleswoman started filling my order.

"You certainly are going to be a lot healthier after you've been eating this for a while," she said.

"Oh, I'm not getting this for me," I said. "It's for my cat."

"Your cat!" She looked over the jars and boxes on the counter. "I think I ought to tell you that you are running up a lot of needless expense. You ought to consider our food supplement designed especially for cats. It contains all the things on the your list and more besides yet costs less."

I bought a bottle of 120 tablets for five dollars. The tablets contain every kind of vitamin from A through E, four kinds of B and enough minerals to start a mine. I also bought a bottle of cod liver oil, all on the advice of Anitra. I also bought some health food chicken and beef.

I hurried home all in a glow, thinking how at last I was doing the right thing for Edith. When I pried the paper off the bottle of supplement tablets, an odor I didn't care for at all smote my nose. The cod liver oil didn't smell good either.

The first morning of the new diet I crushed two tablets of the supplement with the head of a railroad spike and mixed it with a portion of the health food chicken.

Edith ate two bites of chicken. Then she began to paw the floor, covering the dish with imaginary litter.

She then upset the dish of food and sat down in the middle of the mess and glared at me.

The rest of the day every time she passed me, she looked the other way. When I held out a teaspoon of cod liver oil, she sniffed it and walked away.

I tried the vitamin-mineral supplement one more time. Edith immediately set to work covering the stuff.

She was quite willing to eat the unadulterated chicken and beef and even the health-store dry cat food so long as it was flavored with a bit of the junk food she was so happy with before I had read the book. One evening she even jumped up on the table after she finished her dinner and touched her nose to mine.

I figured she had forgiven me for the vitamin supplement.

I really hated to throw away the vitamins and the cod liver oil. I remember when my Irish grandmother died, she left a whole shelf of medicines, some of them prescription and some over-the-counter. My grandfather hated to see all that money go to waste, so although he was in good health, he took all her medicine. It didn't hurt him any so far as we ever knew. I considered taking the vitamin supplement, but if I contracted a rash or something from it, I would hate to explain to my doctor where I got it. So I put the pills and the cod liver oil down the garbage disposer.

After a few months Edith tired of her health food, and I went back to giving her nothing but dry food. Later on I added one small meal of canned meat a day. Some days I bought canned cat food, and other times I bought baby food.

A friend gave me a package of wheat seed and said I should plant it in a pot so that Edith could have a bit of salad now and then during the winter.

One day she came into the office, hopped up on my account book, and eowed.

"What do you want?" I asked. "Show me what you want."

She jumped to the floor and looking over her shoulder to be sure I was following, led me through the kitchen and entry hall into the living room. She hopped up on the table beside her pot of grass.

She made an ineffective attempt to bite off a blade.

"Ow," she said, looking straight at me.

It is difficult for a cat to bite down on a blade of grass. I pulled a blade and held it horizontally across her mouth. She ate it. I picked another blade. She started chewing but looked away in midchew at some imaginary squirrel outside the window.

"Edith," I said, "I have more pressing things to do this morning than to stand here holding your grass while you daydream."

She turned back, finished her blade, and took two more. Then she imagined she saw something on the ceiling and stood gazing at it.

"That's enough salad for today," I said and went back to the office.

I am not sure whether I ought to provide grass for Edith or not.

Frances and Richard Lockridge, who have written a number of books in which their cats appear, say in *Cats and People* that all cats will eat grass if they can find it.

Many people, they say, think that cats should be provided with grass even if the owner has to go to the trouble of raising it.

The Lockridges think that cats fell into the habit of eating grass some millions of years ago, eating it as an emetic to help them get rid of indigestible parts of food they have eaten, such as fur or feathers. It may still be a good idea for feral cats, but for cats who live with people, grass is an irritant they would be better without.

"They do not digest it," say the Lockridges. "If they do not throw it up, which they usually do if they eat it on an empty stomach, it passes through their digestive canal unchanged, except that now and then it clogs the rectum and is often difficult to evacuate. It has no more contact with their 'systems' than so much string would have, and they will also eat string."

The Lockridges had a cat that ate a long piece of string that had been around a rolled rib roast. It came out, they put it, all right in the end. Edith hasn't tried string to my knowledge, but she is death on rubber bands.

Another author thinks the most likely explanation is that cats eat grass to get a chemical they do not get from their regular diet and one they need for health. The chemical is folic acid, which is helpful in the production of hemoglobin. A cat that is deficient in folic acid may become anemic.

I don't know quite where to stand on the grass question. I have seen Edith make swipes at it outdoors. I suppose I will continue to keep growing a little plot of it in the house during the winter.

At an arts festival I met Barb Blaumen, a potter, who makes among other works of art beautiful ceramic bowls with a lovely border and a picture of a cat. I never did like Edith to drink from plastic. I don't eat from plastic and see no reason why she should. She had been using some of my good china.

Barb is a cat person, and she volunteered to make a special bowl for Edith with her name on it.

When the dish was ready, she brought it around to the house to get a look at the most famous cat in our town. Edith was friendly and rolled over to have her stomach rubbed.

After a while she walked over to her scratching post, gave it two rakes, and then lay down in the sunshine.

"I think I ought to tell you," Barb said, "that I believe Edith has a tapeworm."

"A tapeworm? A tapeworm! My gosh, what makes you think so?"

"I saw a little white something on her back end. That's a sure sign."

I was appalled.

As soon as Barb left, I grabbed my cat encyclopedia.

"Internal parasites are common ailments of cats," the book said. "Even the most responsible and meticulous owner cannot always shield his or her cat from infection."

The book went on to say that if you find near your cat's tail a cream-colored segment that looks like a grain of rice, the cat indeed has a tapeworm.

I tried to get a good look under Edith's tail. She wasn't much for having it inspected, but sure enough, I found a little grain of rice. I brushed it off and put it in an envelope.

By the time of her appointment in Dr. Coatney's office, I had five grains in the envelope.

"She has a tapeworm, all right," he said after he looked into the envelope. "She probably got it from eating fleas or a mouse. We'll have her cured in no time."

Then he looked at me and laughed.

"You are the only person who has ever brought me tapeworm samples."

Considering Edith's gastronomic history and what happened next, I believe she has an invincible digestive system.

The first time she ate a chipmunk, she ate skin, paws, bones, tail and all. After that, judging from what I found in the yard, she ate only the meaty portions.

She has a toy made out of a denim bow about two inches by one, tied on a string. I drag the string for Edith to chase. One day I rubbed some fresh catmint on the bow and dangled it in front of her nose. She grabbed at it and I pulled.

A number of times she grabbed at the bow, held it on the floor and bit at it while I pulled on the string. Sometimes it flew out of her grasp, but she nailed it on the next swing past her nose.

All at once I found myself holding a piece of string. Edith had nipped it in two. What is more, the bow had disappeared.

I looked all around the floor in hopes, but the bow was gone, right down into Edith's interior. I grabbed her up and opened her mouth, hoping to find a frayed bit I could get hold of. There were no frayed bits.

Dr. Coatney's office was closed for lunch.

At one o'clock the office secretary said to bring her in.

Edith fussed about getting into her carrying case and howled about riding in the car.

Dr. Coatney saw her right away when he came back from lunch. He felt her but could find no lump of bow anywhere.

"Did it have any wire on it?" he asked.

I said I thought not, but of course, I didn't know what was in the knot of the bow.

"If there is wire," he said, "that's a different matter."

He gave me medicine that contained an antibiotic and something else to coat the lining of her stomach and intestines to get rid of the bow. He said to keep her in the house and give her the medicine for five days or until the bow appeared.

Edith seemed fine; her appetite continued unabated and she loved taking her medicine.

The morning after the incident, I hurried downstairs to the litter box to see if anything had happened.

While I was sifting through the litter, Edith came thumping down the steps and hopped into the box. I have never watched her use the litter box. I figured that is a private activity. This time, however, I stayed and she didn't seem to mind but got right down to her purpose. I could tell that the medicine was working but the bow made no appearance.

I kept her in the house, but I never found the bow.

The days I made her stay inside, I took her out for afternoon walks on her leash.

Each day we followed the same route, which was, of course, of Edith's choosing. She walked down the front steps, down the driveway and up Willowgrove hill, stopping every three seconds or so to look around at the terrain.

At the back of the Adirondack Terrace Apartments, she left the road and walked down through the yard between the foundation bushes and the building walls. Then she headed for a little spinney that faces Patterson Boulevard and sat down to watch the traffic.

That much of the walk took forty-five minutes.

When I began to tire of standing in the apartment lawn holding on to her leash, I picked her up to carry her back home.

She squirmed, shouted, hissed, and dug her claws into my arm. She did not want to go back to the house, and I, big bully that I am, had no right to make her.

Three days of that was as much as either of us could abide.

I never found the bow. Either it disintegrated or she got rid of it outdoors when she returned to her freedom.

On her way home one afternoon Willa stopped her car when she saw me bending over a weed on the hill. She rolled down her car window. "I'm afraid I'm in trouble," she told me.

"What's that?"

"I was working at my desk this morning when Edith appeared in the window and said she wanted to come in," she said. "She often does that, you know. So I opened the door."

When Edith calls on Willa, she follows a routine. She walks from room to room to see whether anything new has been added since she was last there. Then she settles down wherever Willa is working.

"I noticed Edith was playing with something under the desk," Willa continued.

"She kept reaching her paw under the desk and pulling it back. I thought, 'Oh, dear, is there a bug or a mouse under there?'

"I got down on the floor and reached under. Edith had found a big rubber band. I pulled it out, and she tried to get it away from me. I told her I thought she ought not to have it and put it up on a table."

Later Willa went into the kitchen. Shortly afterwards Edith came out and told Willa she wanted to go home.

Willa opened the door.

When she went back to her desk, she noticed that the rubber band had disappeared. On the floor she found half of it.

"I'm terribly worried," she said. "Do you think she swallowed it?"

"I suspect she did," I answered. I told her about the time Edith ate six and coughed them up.

"Oh, dear. Do you think she might have to have surgery?"

"I think she'll probably cough it up if she swallowed it. I'll keep an eye on her, and if she starts acting sick, I'll take her to the vet."

"Be sure to let me know," said Willa. "I'll see to it she gets no more rubber bands in our house."

Next morning I found Edith flattened out on the floor, her head swinging from side to side. She coughed and coughed. Nothing came up. After a time she sat up, rubbed her mouth with her paw, and left on some errand of her own.

I never did find the rest of the rubber band.

Wider World

My gardening friend, Marie Aull, came out of her library with a small book in her hand.

"Have you read this?" she asked, handing me the slim volume.

It was *My Summer in a Garden*, by Charles Dudley Warner.

I hadn't.

"Take it home, then," she said. "You will find something of particular interest in it."

That was how I met Calvin.

My Summer in a Garden is what the title implies, a little book of essays on gardening. Calvin was a feline member of the Warner household for eight years and after he died, Warner wrote an essay about his character. The essay was included by Warner's publisher in a reprint of the garden book, and although the essay was written in 1880, it has been reprinted many times. The book is now out of print, but the essay on Calvin has been reprinted in many cat anthologies.

Calvin first belonged to Harriet Beecher Stowe. "He walked into her house one day, out of the great unknown," Warner wrote, "and became at once at home, as if he had always been a friend of the family. He appeared to have artistic and literary tastes, and it was as if he had inquired at the door if that was the residence of the author of *Uncle Tom's Cabin*, and upon being assured that it was, had decided to dwell there. This is, of course, fanciful for his antecedents were wholly unknown; but in his time he could hardly have been in any household where he would not have heard *Uncle Tom's Cabin* talked about."

After some years Mrs. Stowe, who spent her winters in Florida, gave Calvin to the Warners.

"The intelligence of Calvin was something phenomenal in his rank of life," Warner wrote. "He established a method of communicating his wants and even some of his sentiments; and he could help himself in many things. There was a furnace register in a retired room where he used to go when he wished to be alone, that he always opened when he desired more heat; but never shut it any more than he shut the door after himself. He could do almost everything but speak; and you could declare sometimes that you could see a pathetic longing to do that in his intelligent face. I have no desire to overdraw his qualities, but if there was one thing in him more noticeable than another, it was his fondness for nature. He could content himself for hours at a low window, looking into the ravine and at the great trees, noting the smallest stir there; he delighted, above all things, to accompany me walking in the garden, hearing the birds, getting the smell of the fresh earth, and rejoicing in the sunshine. He followed me and gambolled like a dog, rolling over on the turf and exhibiting his delight in a hundred ways. If I worked, he sat and watched me, or looked off over the bank, and kept his ear open to the twitter in the cherry trees. When it stormed, he was sure to sit at the window, keenly watching the rain or the snow, glancing up and down at its falling, and a winter tempest always delighted him."

Another characteristic of Calvin is one that everyone who has a cat has experienced.

"There was one thing he never did," observed Warner. "He never rushed through an open doorway. He never forgot his dignity. If he had asked to have the door opened and was eager to go out, he always went deliberately; I can see him now, standing on the sill, looking about at the sky as if he was thinking whether it were worthwhile to take an umbrella, until he was near having his tail shut in."

Calvin lived and died more than a century ago, but his story is as fresh and lively as Edith, who lies curled asleep on the desk as I write. His story is universal because cats themselves are.

Carl Van Vechten said that Warner's essay on Calvin "is a masterpiece of sympathetic prose and one of the best cat portraits given to us by a literary man."

Van Vechten, himself a literary man, was also a great admirer of cats. In *Tiger in the House* he wrote, "(The cat) is beautiful and he is graceful. He makes his appearance and his life as exquisite as circumstances will permit. He is modest, he is urbane, he is dignified. Indeed, a well-bred cat never argues. He goes about doing what he likes in a well-bred superior manner. If he is interrupted, he will look at you in mild surprise or silent reproach, but he will return to his desire. If he is prevented, he will wait for a more favorable occasion. But like all well-bred individualists, and unlike human anarchists, the cat seldom interferes with other people's rights. His intelligence keeps him from doing many of the fool things that complicate life. Cats never write operas and they never attend them. They never sign papers or pay taxes or vote for president. An injunction will have no power whatever over a cat. A cat, of course, would not only refuse to obey any amendment whatever, he would refuse to obey the constitution itself."

Isn't that the essence of catness?

Artists have painted cats, sculptors have carved them out of stone and wood, potters have molded them, musicians have translated their voices into fugues and toccatas, poets have described and eulogized them, novelists and essayists have woven stories about them in every land and every language since almost sixteen hundred years before Christ.

The joys of having a cat in the house are unending, and the pleasures of discovering other cats through the eyes of other owners is almost as great. I hesitate at using the word "owner" because nobody can really own a cat. To speak of owning a cat is as bad as the choice of a word by the unknown writer of Genesis. Marie Aull pointed out to me one day that the passage in that book never should have said man was given dominion over the animals.

"The word should have been one that indicates man was appointed to have the care of animals, to be a conservator, not to wield life and death power over them," she said. She would like to have the Bible changed, but she has not succeeded so far.

All lovers of cats are united in a federation of admiration with one another and with those who have gone before them back to the beginning of history.

Nelson Antrim Crawford, a writer about cats and a cat story anthologist, pointed out that cats are the oldest domesticated animal in the world.

"Probably no living creature," he wrote, "has received more extraordinary kindness, even reverence from mankind (it has also received abuse); and no living creature has given more toward making human life more civilized."

Shelves of libraries are filled with books about cats — care of cats, history of cats, cats in art, stories about cats, and anthologies of cat literature. Cat lovers will find reading these books add greatly to the enjoyment of having a cat.

Often I have been struck by the beauty of Edith's eyes, globes of green and gold. In the bright sun the black pupils shrink to slits, but when she sits by my chair, looking up in appeal to open the door, the glowing, round, eloquent pupils nearly blot out all vestiges of color.

Many poets have written about their cats' eyes.

Joachim du Bellay saw many colors in his cat's eyes:

Eyes of a tempered warmth,
Whose pupils of dark green
Showed every color seen

In the bow which splendidly
Arches rainy sky.

John Keats had a cat whose eyes gazed:

With those bright languid segments green

Charles Baudelaire, a famous French writer and cat lover, describes his cat's eyes thus:

And glints of gold, as in a shady stream,
Vaguely bestar their eyeballs mystical.

Lines of Matthew Arnold on his cat's eyes are:

Cruel, but composed and bland,
Dumb, inscrutable and grand.

He added a couplet that has become widely quoted:

So Tiberius might have sat,
Had Tiberius been a cat.

Arnold's fellow Victorian poet, Algernon Charles Swinburne, described his cat's eyes as:

Glorious eyes that smile and burn
Golden eyes, love's lustrous meed.

Rosamund Marriott Watson had a cat:

With somber sea-green eyes inscrutable

Here is William Butler Yeats:

> *Does Minnaloushe know that his pupils*
> *Will pass from change to change*
> *And that from round to crescent*
> *From crescent to round the range?*
> *Minnaloushe creeps through the grass*
> *Alone, important and wise,*
> *And lifts to the changing moon*
> *His changing eyes.*

Edith's eyes are translucent emerald pied with gold. When she lifts then to me in supplication to fill her bowl or open the door, all her being stands in those eyes, pleading and eloquent.

The White and the Blue

One morning I heard a squeal. I thought it was the wailing noise brakes make when they are unable to keep a car from creeping downhill.

There was no car on our hill.

When the wail came again, I opened the front door.

Under one of the porch chairs lay a white cat about half the size of Edith. She had blue eyes and wore a blue collar to match.

Crouching on the other chair was Edith, and the wail was coming from her.

I stepped out on the porch. The white cat moved under a viburnum. Edith crept to the edge of the porch and crouched down facing the white cat, her tail switching back and forth.

Edith wailed in a soprano voice; the white cat wailed three tones lower.

They stared at each other for fifteen minutes, the wailing rising in crescendo and falling away into quiet growling. Finally Edith tucked her tail around her body and settled down. The white cat tucked in her paws and closed her eyes, opening them now and then to peek at Edith.

At last Edith looked at me and at the door. "Do you want to go in?" I asked.

She did.

When Edith disappeared, the white cat came back onto the porch and rolled over on her back, waving her paws in the air.

I picked her up and held her on my lap for a long time. She was half grown and a perky little thing. She pricked her ears forward and watched the traffic pass by. I think we could have sat there all morning.

Finally I put her down, and she took Edith's regular path around the house. The last I saw of her, she was walking up the hill on Willowgrove.

I went into the house and looked up a chapter on cat language.

The wailing noise is called caterwauling. Male cats who know a receptive female is in the neighborhood make it. Two females caterwaul when they engage in a property dispute. Edith's wail meant, "Move on or I will attack you."

The white cat's wail meant, "I am afraid of you, but don't push me too far or I will fight."

Desmond Morris said in *Catlore* that when two cats confront each other, the submissive one will close its eyes to blot out the image of its dominant rival. The other views this as a sign of capitulation and generally calms down. Edith must have read the book. That is why she indicated to me that she was ready to go into the house.

In the afternoon the wailing broke out again at the back of the house. Edith lay on the gravel and the white cat crouched above her on top of the air conditioner. When she saw me, she rolled over on her back and waved her paws. I picked her up and took her into the house, leaving Edith outside with an astonished look on her face.

Edith had left a dish of food, and the white cat ate it all. When Edith came into the house a little later, she paused on the threshold, her tail fluffing out to three times its normal size.

The cats confronted each other in the living room, and we had another duet. After a long time the white cat slunk away, her tail dragging. She disappeared somewhere in the house.

I left one of the garage doors open and after a long time, I saw her walking down the driveway and up

Willowgrove. I never saw her again.

Next-door neighbor Willa became the foster grandmother to Mischa, a young Russian Blue. She asked me whether I thought Edith would like a companion while she and her husband went away for two weeks.

I suggested that Willa should bring her over to the house for a trial visit.

The books say that when introducing a new cat into a household, the cat should be brought in by someone outside the household. They suggest keeping the new cat in a separate room for a while or in a cage to let the resident cat get used to the idea. The resident cat must be assured that the new cat is meant for her or his pleasure and companionship and will never be half so important in the household.

We followed the book instructions. There was one problem: Edith had not read the book.

Mischa stayed in a cage on the porch for the better part of a day. There was howling and yowling and spitting, but after several hours, Edith seemed to have settled down and even put an amiable look on her face. I let Mischa walk from the screened-in porch into the house.

No tornado ever struck quicker than Edith.

Pow! This is my house, you Russian Blue, you. Out! Out! Out!

Mischa disappeared.

Mischa disappeared for hours. I looked under the beds, under the dressers, in all the boxes in the basement, under the car in the garage, in every drawer and closet. I called Willa, who came over and looked, too. Mischa had vanished as if she had never been.

I called Catharine, who found Edith the time she disappeared into the insulation. She even looked behind all the books in the bookcases. She looked everywhere I had looked.

At last she found Mischa in the basement behind the washing machine.

We extracted her, howling and hissing.

We decided that it would be better for Mischa to go back to Willa's house, and I would look after her while they were gone by going in twice a day, getting her food, cleaning the litter box, and playing with her for awhile.

The Hedricks left Sunday morning. Sunday afternoon I went into the house and called Mischa. She did not appear. I left fresh water and food for her and cleaned her litter box.

I did not see her on Monday, but I could tell she had eaten the food. She had not used the litter box.

I did not see her on Tuesday. On Wednesday morning she came down the stairs and hissed at me. On Thursday she was waiting for me and let me pet her a little. We played for a little while, and then I put on her leash and took her outdoors. The truth was that Mischa had not used the litter box all week, and I was worried. I had hopes that she might find the great outdoors litter box to her liking.

She seemed to enjoy prowling over the yard and looking into hollow logs. Nothing I hoped for happened.

On Friday when I arrived, she rushed out from somewhere, rubbed against my legs and rolled over on her back. I patted her stomach. When I suggested a walk outdoors, she held quite still while I snapped on her leash and could hardly wait for me to get the door open.

She was investigating a curled-up leaf when she grew tense. Looking toward the stone steps at the side of the house, she let out a mighty yowl and began hissing.

Crouched on the top step, her ears flattened against her head, her tail switching from side to side lay Edith.

Edith started to advance on Mischa, paw by paw.

I bent to pick Mischa up.

Edith charged.

Mischa raced off through a patch of pachysandra with me galloping at the other end of her leash. If Mischa hadn't run into a corner of the stonewall, we might have been running yet. I grabbed her and escaped into the house.

That was the end of our walks outdoors.

Mischa never did use the litter box the whole two weeks. I found some of the places she had been using and left the rest for Willa to discover when she returned.

One morning when I opened the door to Willa's knock, Edith stepped out onto the porch.

She stalked past Willa without a syllable and sat down at the end of the porch, her tail switching back and forth.

"Good morning, Edith," said Willa, walking to the end of the porch and bending over to stroke her.

Edith stood up, arched her back, fluffed out her tail and stalked six feet farther off to the top of the stone steps.

"Edith, what is wrong with you?" I asked. "I've never seen you act like that before."

"She's angry with me," said Willa. "She hasn't been over to visit since we came back from vacation. I think she is annoyed because we have Mischa. I suppose she can smell her on my hands and clothes."

"Edith," I called. "Come here."

Edith looked around at me without moving.

"Edith, come here. I want to talk with you."

She walked slowly toward me.

"What do you mean, treating Willa like that? Willa is your friend. You hurt her feelings. Now I want you to go over there and tell her that you're sorry."

Edith walked to Willa, looked up, said "Ow" and lay down on her back for Willa to rub her stomach.

I took her into the house and gave her a treat.

After lunch Edith walked over to Willa's house and found her working in her perennial bed, which is on top of a stone ledge. She walked along the ledge right up to Willa, rubbed her cheek against Willa's and purring loudly, lay right down in the iberis for another stomach rub.

"I accepted her apology," said Willa.

Since then Mischa has gone to live with another family that doesn't go away very often, and Edith went on to the most harrowing adventure she has had so far.

Adirondack Ordeal

As Edith grew older, she developed fairly regular habits. She leaves the house at six o'clock in the morning for her early constitutional.

An hour later she comes back for her second breakfast. If it is a nice day, she goes out again for the morning. If it is cold or rainy, she takes a nap on the harpsichord.

She comes home or gets up for lunch. She spends the afternoon visiting the neighbors, comes home for dinner, goes out once more for an evening walk, and then comes home for the night.

One Wednesday morning she left at six as usual.

She did not come home for breakfast.

She did not come home for lunch.

She did not come for dinner or at bedtime.

Every hour all night long I went to the door. She was never there.

A few times Edith has stayed out all night. But except for the time she was kidnapped, she has always been waiting on the porch in the morning.

Edith was not on the porch in the morning. I knew then that if she could come home, she would.

Anybody who has ever had a cat knows what a devastating feeling it is when the cat is missing.

Imagination runs wild. One sees the cat lying mangled in the street, mewed up in someone's garage, caught in a culvert, slaughtered by dogs — oh, there's no end to the grim possibilities.

I had just read in SICSA's newsletter that someone brought an old, blind cat to the pet adoption center. He was given a cage and although staff members and volunteers petted him and talked to him every time they passed his cage, he did not respond.

Every time a door opened, however, or the telephone rang or somebody spoke, he cocked his head and listened, his blind eyes staring straight ahead. He seemed to respond more to men's voices than to women's, and the staff concluded that somewhere a man was grieving for his lost pet just as Blind Bob, as they called him, was grieving.

One volunteer drove to the area where he had been found, posted signs on the telephone poles and knocked on many doors, but the trip was in vain. SICSA put an ad in the newspaper, but nobody called. Another volunteer called the Humane Society. "Has anybody inquired of you about a lost black cat, blind and very old?"

Yes, an elderly man had inquired about just such a cat, but nobody knew his name or address. He had also called the Montgomery County Animal Shelter.

"We'll keep the ad running in the paper a few more days," Alice Lavery, the SICSA head, decided. "Maybe he doesn't take the daily paper but will see it in the Sunday paper."

That is exactly what happened. He called early Sunday morning.

He came to SICSA at once, and when Blind Bob heard his voice, he jumped up in his cage and began meowing with such evident joy that everybody watching the reunion of the two could not keep back the tears.

As soon as SICSA opened, I telephoned. No, Edith wasn't there, but they would let me know if somebody brought her in. I called the street department and showed her picture to my mailman. I put an ad in the lost and found department of the newspaper.

I tramped the neighborhood. I telephoned Catharine.

"Maybe she's been kidnapped again," she said. "Could her collar be caught on something? You always check to see it is not too loose when you put it on her, don't you?"

"Yes. She's wearing her yellow collar."

"I'll come over after lunch. We know where she usually goes."

I washed up Edith's dishes and put them on the counter. I felt like a traitor having lunch when she wasn't having any wherever she was.

While I ate a poached egg, I read an anthology of cat poetry.

Poets have been writing about their cats for centuries. Thomas Gray wrote "Death of a Favorite Cat, Drown'd in a Tub of Gold Fishes." William Cowper wrote in "The Retired Cat" how his kitten, who'd crept into an open drawer to sleep, was shut in overnight by the chambermaid. William Wordsworth wrote "The Kitten and the Falling Leaves"; Percy Bysshe Shelley called his poem simply "Verses for a Cat"; John Keats composed a sonnet to a cat, and Matthew Arnold's "Atossa" is in many an anthology. Christina Rossetti, Seumas O'Sullivan, Harold Munro, Swinburne, Thomas Hardy, Yeats, Edmond Rostand, Walter de la Mare, Lytton Strachey, William Rose Benet, T.S. Eliot, Victoria Sackville-West, Dorothy L. Sayers — the list of poets who wrote about cats could fill up this page.

Many of the poems were about cats who had died.

As I read, I thought about Moonbeam, whose path worn through the ivy by his little black feet has become invisible in the new green leaves. How could I bear it if I never saw Edith again?

The more I read, the sadder I became. Then I heard Catharine's car in the driveway and closed the book.

Together we walked through the back yards of all the houses in the neighborhood.

No Edith came to our call. At one place Catharine stopped. "There's a cat in that house," she said. "I can hear it. Don't you hear it?"

I couldn't hear a thing.

"Maybe Edith walked in when somebody opened the door to get the paper. Let's ask."

We rang and rang, but nobody answered the door.

I knocked on the door of the next house.

"Oh, those people both work," said the woman who answered. "They do have a cat, though. They never let her out. She's very old."

We walked on, looking in brush piles and compost heaps until we were far from Edith's haunts.

At last we went back home.

"We didn't walk up Willowgrove," said Catharine.

"I walked up there yesterday afternoon."

"Let's go up there again. You know you don't hear very well. I've often seen her taking a nap right in the middle of Willowgrove."

"She thinks it's her street."

We set off up the hill, calling.

As we passed the house next door, Catharine stopped and held up her hand.

"I hear a cat. Edith!"

We listened.

"She answered. It's Edith. I recognize her voice."

We walked to the Adirondack Apartments.

"She's somewhere around here," Catharine said. "Look in the bushes. Edith!"

"Ow!"

Even I heard her that time.

Peering over the edge of a roof three stories above us was Edith.

"How in the world did she ever get up there?"

Catharine pointed to a tree switching in the wind.

"She climbed that tree and jumped. But with that wind, she couldn't jump back."

"How will we ever get her down?"

Edith peered over the edge of the roof and we could tell she was thinking about jumping, but it was too high.

There was a window directly under Edith.

"Maybe you could get into that apartment and stand in the window and reach up for her," said Catharine.

"Let's go see," I said.

We walked into the apartment and up three flights of stairs. I knocked on the door of the one I figured was under Edith.

A young man opened the door. I told him about Edith.

"I can get on the roof," he said. "I have a key because sometimes I go up there to sunbathe. Wait till I get my shoes on."

He was at home from classes at the university, he explained, working on a paper. "My name's Dick Elder," he said.

He took a key off a hook and walked down half a flight of steps. He opened a door and revealed a ladder flat against the wall. Up the ladder he climbed some twenty feet. I stood at the bottom and watched him open a trap door and disappear.

"Her name is Edith," I called.

After a while he poked his head through the trap door opening.

"She comes close to me," he called down, "but then when I reach for her, she backs away."

"She'll come to me," said Catharine. She took off her jacket and up the ladder she went.

"Wow, this is horrible," she shouted when she reached the top. "There isn't anything to hold on to."

I stood down below, looking up at the patch of blue sky.

Dick backed down the ladder.

"She came right to your friend," he said. "I have a knapsack. I'll put Edith in it and strap it on my back."

He took the knapsack up.

"She won't stay in it," he called after a little while.

"I have an idea," I said. "Get a pillowcase and put her in it. Tie it shut and put it in the knapsack."

They stuffed a yowling Edith into the pillowcase. He put her into the knapsack and backed down the ladder.

He handed me the knapsack, and I opened the pillowcase far enough for Edith to poke her head out. She looked at me and I swear a look of relief spread over her face.

Meanwhile Catharine faced the problem of how to get down off the roof. There was no handhold on the ladder, which ended flush at the roof edge. She had to lie on her stomach, ease her legs through the opening and wiggle her feet in the air until she could locate a ladder rung. Then she reached down for the second rung with her other foot, still holding onto the rough roof with her bare hands.

With help from Dick, she finally made it.

"I'll never do that again," she said when she finally reached the floor. "That's a twenty-foot drop onto concrete. I could have cracked my skull or broken a leg. And don't you ever try it if she goes up on that roof again. You couldn't make it. Your legs are too long."

Dick's pillowcase was filthy. After all, Edith had been mopping up that dirty roof for almost two days and one night. We volunteered to take the pillowcase home and wash it, but he laughed and said it was laundry day anyhow. He wouldn't take a reward.

At home Edith ate a good meal, drank some water, and started in to give herself a good washing.

I found an unopened fifth of Jack Daniels in the liquor cabinet, and Catharine and I took it over to Dick.

"Don't you ever do that again," I said to Edith when we came back.

"She probably will," said Catharine.

I think she will not. So far Edith has never made the same mistake twice.

Stressed Out

When Edith sleeps, she is so relaxed that nothing disturbs her — not a television bleating, not conversation around her, not a hand stroking her fur. She lies on her side with her legs and her tail stretched out as far as they can go or on her back with her forepaws tucked like little hands on her chest.

Often I look at her sleeping and think that nothing can ever disturb her tranquility.

But I was wrong.

Edith in her fifth year became a victim of stress. It began because of something I did.

One Sunday morning she ate half her breakfast and went out to check her real estate on Springhill Avenue. Something must have required investigation in depth because she had not returned by ten o'clock, when it was time for me to leave for church.

On Sundays I come home after lunch, but that Sunday I went out to look at spring in Marie Aull's garden and did not return until a little after four o'clock. That's a long time for a cat who has had only half her breakfast.

I don't like to leave Edith outdoors when I go away, but when I do, she is almost always waiting on the porch when I come home. The moment the car swings into the driveway, she comes bounding down the steps, lies down on her back in the driveway, paws in the air, and I give her a stomach rub. Then she rolls over, stands up, hoists her tail like a ship's mast, and follows me into the garage. While I unlock the door into the laundry room, she rubs against my ankles.

On this Sunday she came down the steps, but I could tell right away by the look on her face something was wrong. I stepped out of the car to give her the stomach roll, but she walked straight past me with never an indication that she knew I was there. She set each paw down with a deliberate stomp, and her tail dragged the ground. I think she was humming the death march from *Saul* as she marched.

I stood in the garage doorway.

"Edith, aren't you coming in for some lunch?"

Usually the word "lunch" will bring her from as far away as the ninth tee at Community Golf club, but this time she stalked down the driveway, crossed Willowgrove, and sat down with her back to me, staring into her private jungle that flourishes at the end of our lot.

"Edith, are you coming in?"

She stared into the jungle.

"Edith!"

She turned her head around and glared at me. I could read implacable contempt all over her face.

"You go away without letting me know," she seemed to say. "I waited and waited so I could finish my breakfast. You didn't come back all morning, and I had to go without my lunch. You had your lunch, no doubt, and never gave me a thought. Don't think you can come back now that you are good and ready and expect me to fall all over you with joy."

She turned back to her contemplation of the jungle.

"All right, Edith. I'll leave the door ajar. You come in when you're ready."

A few minutes later I heard her running up the steps and then the clink of her name tag against her food dish. As soon as she finished eating, she disappeared.

She reappeared at dinnertime. After dinner she usually sits on my lap to watch the evening news on TV, but this time she walked to the door and waited for me to open it, stepped out onto the porch without a word, and did not come back until bedtime. Ordinarily she sleeps on the foot of my bed, but this time she spent the night in her chair in the living room. She didn't sit on my lap for three months after that. She knows how to hold a grudge.

Soon after she had her feelings hurt, several other events made matters worse.

She stopped eating with her usual gusto and lost interest in going outdoors, preferring to sleep all morning and all afternoon in her chair in the living room.

Dr. Coatney checked her ears, eyes, teeth, and body. He discovered that she had a kidney infection. He said that he had been seeing a great many cats about that time, all with kidney infections. He thought the unusual changes in atmospheric pressure caused stress, which brought on infection.

Edith was slow in recovering. Usually she loves taking medicine, but this time she hated it. Every time she saw me get out the bottle, she ran under the bed. It is very hard to get a cat out from under a bed.

She became worse. I took her back to see Dr. Coatney. She had a temperature of 104 (101 is normal for a cat).

"I believe she has developed a resistance to this particular brand of antibiotic," he said. "I'm going to switch her to sulfa."

He gave her a shot, cautioned me to see that she drank plenty of water, and gave me a different kind of medicine.

She seemed to get worse. This time when we went back to the vet, she had a temperature of 106.

"This is serious," Dr. Coatney said. "She is going to need a shot every day for a while. I think we'd better keep her in the hospital until we can get her fever under control."

She was there four days and nights. When I brought her home, she was so happy she ran up the steps two at a time. She liked her new medicine, too.

Her happiness, however, was short-lived.

For a long time I wanted to get new carpet. The carpet that was in the house when I bought it was the kind that showed traffic marks that would not come out with cleaning.

Tom Harmon had brought samples of new carpet several months before. Edith happened to be in the house when he came, and she inspected every sample of carpet. I picked out one called "muted mauve," which went very well with the wallpaper, the tile on the kitchen floor, and Edith's colors.

The day after Edith came home from the hospital, Tom telephoned to say that he would be coming the next morning to lay the carpet. It would take two days.

Edith stayed outdoors most of the time while the furniture was moved around and the carpet laid.

When the carpet was down, I could see at once that the old upholstered furniture in the living room would not do. The colors were all wrong. What is more, Edith's scratching post was the wrong color, too. Tom took it home to recover it with some new carpet.

I gave away the two love seats and the old wing chair Edith had claimed for her own shortly after she moved here.

In their place stands a pale ivory brocaded sofa and chair. I thought Edith would be pleased to have a nice, new sofa to snooze on.

She sniffed the new carpet and the new furniture.

She would have none of it.

She slept on the hard but familiar tile floor in the kitchen. She had to walk on the new carpet to leave by the front or back door, but every time she stepped on it, she glared at me.

Three days after the furniture was delivered, Blackwell came to stay for a week while her people went to Vermont. She immediately staked out the end of the sofa as hers, where she lay like Cleopatra on her barge floating down the Nile. Edith probably could have coped with Blackwell, but with her also came Calvin, a twelve-week-old black kitten Blackwell's people had adopted.

When she saw Calvin, Edith's fur rose along her backbone, her tail fluffed out like a brush, and her growls made me shiver. I had to confine Calvin to Edith's basement jail room.

It was no fun for a kitten to live by himself in the basement. For two days I raced up and down steps, letting Calvin out whenever Edith went outdoors and hurrying him to jail whenever I saw Edith out on the porch wanting to come in. One morning when Edith was eating breakfast I slipped downstairs to give Calvin some food and forgot to close the door.

You know how it is when you feel someone staring at you. I turned around and there stood Edith. She looked as if she could not understand why I had that kitten downstairs. Her fur fluffed up and she growled, and this time it was not only at Calvin but at me also.

I told Willa about my problems, and she agreed to take Calvin into her house until the Bookers came home. I fixed up a litter box, a box of food, a few toys, and Calvin's earmite medicine and took them and Calvin to Willa's.

Even with Calvin gone, Edith acted unhappy. She began to lose her appetite and mope around the house.

One morning she went out and visited Willa while she planted some pachysandra. That evening Willa telephoned.

"I'm worried about Edith," she said. "She spent the afternoon with me just lying on the ground watching.

Usually she jumps into every hole I dig. Are you sure she is well?"

"I've noticed she seems listless."

"If it's all right with you, Elvin will make a house call and take her temperature."

"Oh, please do have him come."

Willa's husband is an M.D., not a veterinarian, and ordinarily does not make house calls, but he appeared shortly with thermometer in hand and took Edith's temperature.

He said he thought she'd better have Dr. Coatney look at her in the morning. He gave me the thermometer, but I have found that one person alone cannot take a cat's temperature. Not Edith's, anyhow.

Dr. Coatney was on vacation. Dr. Ralph Stall, one of the doctors who had agreed to take Dr. Coatney's patients, checked Edith and asked whether she was under any stress.

I told him about the furniture and the cats and the kidney problems. He said he thought that Edith was heading right back into another infection. He gave me some more of Edith's pink medicine, which Elvin said was penicillin, and said to take her back to Dr. Coatney as soon as he returned.

That was on Friday. Edith refused to let me give her the medicine. I had to force the medicine dropper between her teeth, and we had pink showers all over the table but not much of it went into Edith.

She continued to exhibit listlessness.

I thought if I could persuade Willa to take Blackwall as well as Calvin, Edith would at least have less stress.

Willa agreed to take Blackwell, and I will say that as soon as Blackwell was out of the house, Edith seemed to improve slightly.

Willa reported trouble at her house. Blackwell thought she ought to sit on the dining room table and walk around on Willa's kitchen counter tops whenever she wanted to. So did Calvin. Willa would not allow either one of them on the table or counter, and what is more she wouldn't let them come into her bedroom at night.

Calvin didn't mind; anything was all right with him, but Blackwell took offense. She sat around, staring at them blackly. Then Calvin started using Blackwell's litter box instead of his own. That made Blackwell angry, so she used Willa's living room carpet. (Willa didn't tell me about that, but she did tell Catharine when she came home, and Catharine told me.)

When Dr. Coatney came back the following Monday, he gave Edith a shot of a different kind of medicine and a bottle of antibiotic that she liked. When it was time for her dose, I filled the medicine dropper and held it out to her. She marched right up and opened her mouth and took it all. By the end of two weeks her health was back to normal.

It was about that time at church a visitor asked me, "What are you going to do when Edith dies?"

I felt as if he had hit me on the chin. I always try to have an answer for every question even if it isn't right, but his time I stood there powerless to speak. I thought plenty, however. What kind of person is so callous as to ask such a question, especially in the parish hall? I don't care if that man never comes back to our church again.

The question did make me think that I ought to make arrangements for Edith in case something dire happened to me.

I called up my lawyer and told him I wanted to leave some money to Edith.

"You mean the Edith I have read about in the paper? Isn't she a cat?"

"Yes, she is. And I do mean that Edith."

There was a silence. "Offhand I would say you can't do that. The court would have to have someone to administer the money, since she obviously wouldn't be able to. But I will look up the law and let you know."

He did, and I have a new will now. One of the provisions is this: If Catharine Booker survives me, I give Edith and $10,000 to Catharine Booker. I request that Catharine Booker provide and maintain a comfortable home for Edith and that she expend such sums as she considers reasonable and appropriate for Edith's care and welfare. I also request that Catharine Booker make suitable financial and other arrangements for Edith's care and welfare after Catharine's death or if Catharine is otherwise unable to provide for Edith.

I also made arrangements for another friend to look after Edith if Catharine does not survive me.

While I was at it, I left money to provide altar flowers once a year in memory of several members of my family, and in the list is the name of Edith McPherson. It pleases me to think that long after we are both gone, parishioners at our church will enjoy the flowers and that Edith will be remembered in their prayers at least one Sunday every year.

The new will solved one problem, but the carpet and the furniture problem remained.

For years we had companionable evenings, Edith lying in the green chair facing me in my chair and the television set. Sometimes she would sit on my lap for an hour or so and then go back to her chair. When she stretched out full length in it, she was too long for the chair's width, but she solved that problem by sleeping on the bias like the hypotenuse of a triangle. She sometimes snoozed curved around her scratching post. When it was my bedtime, I always gave her a pat and said goodnight.

During the night she usually came into the bedroom and either walked across me to get to the other twin bed or slept on the end of mine.

Those companionable evenings vanished with the old carpet and furniture.

I rubbed Edith's newly-covered scratching post with catnip. She can't resist that delicious herb, and she soon began to use as a pillow the little platform that holds the post.

I had thought Edith would use the end of the sofa for napping and watching television and put the towel that had been on the green chair on the sofa. She would have none of it. She lies on the hard kitchen floor or else goes out and naps under the taxus.

I felt bad that I gave Edith's chair away. I gave it to Willa, who is head of the welfare department at our church. I thought of asking for it back, but I was pretty sure the chair had gone into the home of one of the needy families the church helps.

The new sofa is longer than the love seat it replaced, but if I moved the television set farther back in the corner and the potted plant table nearer the television, there might be room for a new wing chair for Edith.

I decided to look around in the shops.

Eight Stitches in Time

One morning when I brushed Edith's coat she cringed and cried when I reached a spot on her left hip. Over the next few days the spot became increasingly sensitive, and I noticed that Edith's old symptoms of kidney infection had returned. She seemed lethargic and her appetite flagged.

Dr. Coatney's sensitive fingers explored the spot. "I think she has an abscess," he said. "She has been scratched by a thorn or another cat and the scratch has become infected." He gave her a shot and sent us home with a bottle of antibiotic medicine.

She was better for a few days, but when the medicine was gone, she became worse. Over several months we tried different antibiotics, but after a time each one became ineffective. The abscess neither went away nor broke open, as Dr. Coatney hoped.

One morning Edith wouldn't eat bite one. When Edith, who is ordinarily a prodigious trencherwoman, stops eating, she is really sick. Dr. Coatney examined her and looked grave. "That infection from the abscess has spread to her kidneys and bladder," he said. "I think it will have to be removed."

She had a high fever. "If you will bring her in every morning for a week," he said, "I will give her a shot to reduce the infection and lower her fever. As soon as we get it down a few degrees, we'll remove the abscess."

I took her to the clinic every morning before his office hours began and after ten days she had only one degree of fever. Then one morning I took a crying, breakfastless Edith in for surgery and spent an endless day until it was time to call in to see how she had fared.

She came through the surgery beautifully. "The abscess was bad," Dr. Coatney reported. "Scar tissue had developed, and it was dark yellow. Antibiotics never would have cured it. I had to go quite deep; she will have a sore hip for a while."

When I brought her home the next afternoon, she seemed subdued and weak. She had a bare spot on her hip as big as your palm and a sutured incision about three inches long.

She was still on twice-daily antibiotics. In a few days she regained her old bounce.

Then one morning I discovered Edith had evidently taken out all the sutures. Dr. Coatney gave me an ointment to apply daily to help the healing. He told me to put it on four or five times a day and then to distract Edith by a game or conversation for at least five minutes to give the medicine a chance to work. He knew she would lick it off.

We kept up this routine for several days.

One night about 10:15 Edith went out for her evening constitutional. She came in a little later and headed straight to her food bowl and began eating. Out of the corner of my eye I saw a flash of red. What could that be? When I investigated, I found blood from the incision running down Edith's leg. It opened completely and a flap of her skin hung down so that I could see right into her anatomy.

I thought I was a calm person in an emergency. I am not. "Oh, Edith, what are we going to do?" I wailed. Wildly I thought about bandaging the wound until morning when Dr. Coatney's office opened. When I opened the cabinet where I kept Edith's first aid kit, I realized that Edith wouldn't stand for a bandage and besides, this was too serious for first aid.

I had three pairs of glasses lying around the house, but I couldn't find a one of them. Without them the telephone is a mystery to me. I stumbled over a magnifying glass I use for the stock market and called Catharine.

She had already gone to bed. "I think you should call Dr. Coatney," she said.

"Oh, I can't. I can't read the phone book. I can't find my glasses. Besides, it's after office hours. She's bleeding. What shall I do?"

"Wrap her in a clean towel," she said. "I will call Dr. Coatney."

I put a towel around Edith, but she walked right out of it and bled on the tablecloth. She seemed not the least upset.

In a few minutes Dr. Coatney called. "How soon can you get to the clinic?" he asked. "I'll meet you there."

Gibralter fell off my shoulders.

I put Edith into the carrying case and drove up Patterson Road to Catharine's house. She had dressed and was ready to go along. Off we went. I was so excited I couldn't tell whether the lights were red or green and I would have missed the turn into the right street, but she kept telling me when to stop, go, and turn. When we arrived, the lights in the clinic were on and Dr. Coatney, the dear man, was waiting.

"My, my," he said when he saw Edith's gaping side. "I'll have to replace those sutures right away. That means a general anesthetic and she will have to stay overnight."

"But she has just eaten," I wailed.

"She will throw up. They always do."

He talked soothingly to her for a little while and then brought out a needle. I held her while he gave her the shot. We patted her and talked to her until she settled down and then he took her away.

Next morning she was ready to come home. When she stepped out of the carrying case, she was unable to walk up the stairs. I carried her up to the kitchen and set her on the floor. She tried to walk, but she was wobbly and she fell over. She got up again and took a few more steps and collapsed. I carried her into her favorite spot by the scratching post and she went to sleep, crouched in the sick cat position with her paws tucked under her and her nose in the carpet. She lay there, unmoving, hour after hour.

Dr. Coatney gave me a bottle of liquid called Bitter Orange to put on the incision four or five times a day so that Edith wouldn't be tempted to take the sutures out.

I tasted it. The taste took me back to the worst experience I had ever had in a dentist's chair — when the doctor rubbed a gum with alum to stop some bleeding. Have you ever tasted alum? Only after you have tasted alum or Bitter Orange can you talk intelligently about the acrid side of life. Gall, wormwood, and quinine are bitter, alum is bitterer and Bitter Orange is bitterest of all. Ugh. Horrible. Your mouth feels as if it is turning inside out.

The eight new sutures looked like the same kind of tough plastic string that merchants use to anchor price tags to sweaters. Yet despite their toughness and the vile taste of Bitter Orange, Edith managed to take out four of the sutures one night. Four more and we would be back for a third stitching.

Dr. Coatney said to bring her in.

He looked at the incision and shook his head. "This calls for drastic measures," he said.

He put a line of Super Glue on the incision. "This should keep it from breaking open," he explained. Then he brought out a three-inch plastic collar and put it around her neck, fastening it to her regular collar. "This will prevent her from reaching the stitches," he said. "If she has trouble eating and drinking, take it off, but be sure to put it back on as soon as she is finished. She must wear this collar for two weeks, until it is time to take out the sutures."

She looked as if she were walking around with her neck in a funnel. The collar edge caught on the furniture and woodwork and stopped her forward progress until she backed up and started again. I had to ask people who came to see her not to laugh, as she was very sensitive about the collar.

It prevented her from giving herself her usual baths, but after a few days she began twisting until she could reach parts of her and even managed to fray out the ends of the stitches. I washed her face with a damp cotton ball.

Three times she took the collar off by putting her paw under the edge and rubbing. She got it off once while Dorothy was at home and I was at work. She wouldn't let Dorothy put it back on, so Dorothy had to stop cleaning to watch that she didn't get at those stitches.

I kept her indoors for a few days at first, but one day she slipped out when I opened the door for a visitor, and a while later I saw her walking up the street looking like a little vacuum sweeper.

After two weeks Dr. Coatney took off the collar and removed the stitches. It would be two months before her fur would grow back again.

Oh, That Edith

Shortly before Edith came, I developed a disease I called Retirement Home Syndrome.

In the past few years retirement communities with nursing home attachments have sprung up all over the country, and men and women have moved into them in great numbers and at great expense.

I had already retired from my five-day-a-week job at the newspaper a year or so before Edith came, although I still have an office there and a weekly column and go to work two mornings a week.

Several of my friends — some of them older than I and one the same age — moved into retirement villages and kept telling me, in euphoric terms, about their new lives. They no longer cooked or cleaned or did laundry or worried about a new roof or patching the driveway. The village bus took them to the theater, concerts, the doctor, shopping centers, and museums. They could join all sorts of clubs right in their own building and make baskets, play cards, and take aerobic dance classes.

I didn't want to do any of those things, but several incidents worried me. In one year's time three of my acquaintances who lived alone had assorted strokes, broken hips, and heart attacks in their homes and were not found for a long time.

"You are living on borrowed time," said my college classmate Grace after she moved into a swanky high-rise home in a Sarasota retirement complex. "You could fall down your basement stairs any day and break your hip. Up on your hill, nobody would find you for ages."

I do live high up on a hill in a house surrounded by forty trees, and she might be right. So I put my name on the waiting list of a village in my end of town.

After Edith came, I forgot about the retirement home and the waiting list. But one morning when Edith was taking a nap on the harpsichord, the letter came. The director of admissions wrote that my name was now on the top of the list and the next vacancy would be mine. She wanted me to drive out and start filling out preliminary papers.

I looked at Edith dreaming away on the harpsichord. Some cat books say that cats like their own territory and do not welcome change. Others say that cats love the human beings who take care of them and will be happy wherever they go, just so they are together. Once when I had the living room painted, I do know that Edith became upset because the men moved the furniture while she was out for her morning constitutional.

Edith loved her constitutional, for she took it every morning, rain, shine, or snow. One morning the ground was snow-covered, and when she left for her hike, she left her paw marks in the snow. For fun I decided to follow her tracks. She went down the front steps to the driveway and down to the honeysuckle tangle across the street from our house. Into the thicket she went. Her tracks emerged some twenty feet up the street. They led up the Willowgrove hill to the Adirondack Terrace Apartments.

The tracks skirted the bushes around the apartment and then went back down Willowgrove on the other side, up the driveway of my next neighbor, and down to the stone wall along the alpine garden. Just behind the fountain she jumped up the second wall into the woods and struck out through the ivy to Willa's house. Then her tracks came down the wooden steps to the upper woods, led behind the viburnum bushes across the front of our house, across the sill of her window, and so to the front porch again.

It would be hard on Edith to leave her pleasant haunts to go with me to a high-rise apartment building. But I intended to take her outdoors every day and roam with her through the parklike gardens and rolling hills of our new home.

Moving into an apartment would probably be harder on me than on Edith. I, too, was used to our woods and hills. I wouldn't have a garden to dig in or a place to cook steaks or hot dogs outdoors. But I wouldn't have to weed, either, and where I was going, I would not have to cook or clean or do laundry. Perhaps we both would learn in time to like our new home.

I drove out to the place, an imposing collection of buildings on acres of rolling land with cottages, an apartment building, and a health care wing for those who could no longer live on their own.

The admissions secretary was a brisk, efficient woman with shiny eyeglasses. I told her I wasn't really sure whether it was time yet for me to move into the village. She said that if I wanted freedom from the cares of home maintenance, from routine chores, from isolation and loneliness, the village was the place for me. I agreed it would be pleasant not to worry about why my water bill was twice the size of my neighbor's, who had more people in her family and twice as big a yard to water as I had. It would be fun not to worry about window-washers, painting, taking care of the humidifier, raking leaves and shoveling snow.

"When you consider the steady, escalating costs of home ownership, rising taxes, and maintenance expenses," she said, "living in our village can be a real bargain. The comfort of knowing that your needs will be met in a planned, dignified, and secure setting is worth a great deal."

She was right about that, and if I broke a hip somebody would be sure to find me pretty soon. The health care center is available to residents, and the nursing service is staffed twenty-four hours a day. Health care teams respond to all emergency calls by residents.

She handed me an agreement to read over. Some of it was about how I would pay the bills and when. Several pages gave what the retirement home would provide.

It told what I as a resident would be responsible for.

I looked down the list.

Stipulation J popped out on the page:

J. Resident understands and will comply with the no-pet policy.

"What's this? You have a no-pet policy?"

"We do not allow pets of any kind."

"But I have a cat," I said. "Edith."

"I know," she said. "I have read about Edith in the paper. You surely won't have any trouble making arrangements for her when you come here. I'm sure you have many friends who would be glad to give her a home."

I sat there like a lump. "Give Edith away?" I finally said. "I would as soon chop off my right hand as give Edith away. Edith is my friend. I am hers."

She smiled. "I know how you feel. I have two cats of my own. But that is the rule. No pets. No exceptions can be made."

I stood up. "Thank you for your time talking with me. I cannot come unless Edith can come, too. If you ever change your policy, perhaps you will let me know."

When I turned into our driveway, Edith came running down Willowgrove, her tail straight up. I picked her up and hugged her.

"Do you know what I am going to do, Edith McPherson?" I asked, carrying her upstairs. "I am going to sit down and figure what I have to do so we can stay here forever and forever and never move to a retirement village. They don't allow cats there."

The first thing I did was to apply for long-term health insurance so that if I break something or fall ill otherwise, I will be able to pay for somebody to come in and look after us.

I arranged to telephone a friend every morning at eight o'clock. If I don't call, he is supposed to investigate. Since he lives alone, too, my call helps him. If he doesn't answer, I will investigate. Willa also told me that if I need help, I should telephone her and she will come right over. So did Catharine.

One day as I took a short cut through the furniture department of a downtown store, I saw the perfect chair for Edith. It was a claret-colored wing chair. Edith would look handsome against the color, and it would go beautifully with the mauve carpet. Its texture and construction were firm, and the seat exactly the right shape for a cat sleeping on the hypotenuse.

"Have you tried sitting in the chair?" Gloria, the saleswoman asked.

"Well, no. You see it really isn't for me. It's for Edith."

"Perhaps you ought to have her try it out."

"Oh, I think it will fit."

"You can never tell about another person," Gloria said. "I've had a lot of experience in this business and more than once we have had to exchange a chair because the person for whom it was intended hadn't tried it out."

"Edith is my cat."

Gloria gave me a startled look. "In that case," she suggested, "perhaps you ought to have it treated for stain resistance."

Edith was out the day the chair was delivered. When she came in and had her snack, I called her into the living room to see her new chair. She sniffed at the corners of it and walked away. I set her in it, but she hopped out of it and went for another snack.

Catharine came to see the chair. "She probably will never sit in it," she said, "because it isn't where her old green chair was. Cats do not like change of any kind."

The room wouldn't look as nice if I moved everything around to put the new wing chair where the old one had been.

That is where matters stood for a long time. I wanted Edith to sit in the chair where it is, and she didn't want to.

Then something happened that changed both our lives.

Greener Pastures

I t began when a legislator, Representative Jim Davis of St. Mary's, Ohio, introduced a bill into the Ohio State Legislature to license cats and to require owners to keep their pets on their own property. The bill provided that the owner of a licensed cat wandering free and picked up by a neighbor or the police would be subject to a two hundred dollar fine, and unlicensed cats would be turned over to laboratories for medical experiments.

Cat owners all over the state rose up in anger and pelted every letter-to-the-editor page in the state with outcries. Many did not object to buying a license, especially if the money realized went to improve conditions for cats through spaying and neutering and to underwrite cat shelters, but anybody who knows cats understands that even if cats understood boundaries, they would pay no attention to them. The animal rights activists were particularly vocal about the medical experiments.

Twice before, state legislatures have undertaken to license cats, once in California and once in Illinois. Both pieces of legislation failed. The law did pass the senate in Illinois and went to the desk of the then-governor, Adlai E. Stevenson.

He vetoed the bill, and his letter explaining his veto earned him a place in many a cat literature anthology.

"I cannot agree that a cat visiting a neighbor's yard or crossing the highway is a public nuisance," he said. "It is in the nature of the cat to do a certain amount of unescorted roaming."

He pointed out that it is also against the nature of a cat's owner to escort abroad a cat on a leash. Cats also perform useful services, particularly in rural areas, in combating rodents — works they necessarily perform alone and without regard to property lines.

"The problem of cat vs. bird is as old as time," he continued. "If we attempt to resolve it by legislation, who knows but what we may be called upon to take sides as well as the age-old problem of dog vs. cat, bird vs. bird, or even bird vs. worm. In my opinion the state of Illinois has better things to do without trying to control feline delinquency."

I worried that if the bill passed our legislature and went to the governor's desk, he might not know about the precedent set by Stevenson and sign the bill. I wrote a column to have ready to send him in case the bill passed.

I had also just heard about the experience of Ruth Oltman, a college classmate. Ruth had lived happily for many years with her cat, but finally arthritis made it impossible for her to drive her car any longer, and she moved into a retirement home. The rules of the home forbade her to bring her cat with her, and she had to find a friend who was willing to give her cat a home. Ruth grieved at parting with her dearly loved friend.

Two years later she had to be hospitalized briefly at a place distant from the retirement home but near the farm home of her friends who took her cat. When it was time for Ruth to leave the hospital, her friends offered to drive her back to her apartment. They did not take the direct route, however, but detoured by way of their farm. When Ruth's cat saw her, she ran and leaped into Ruth's arms with joyous cries. For an hour Ruth sat with the cat purring on her lap as they had so many times in the old days.

At last the return could be delayed no longer, and for a second time the two had to part. Ruth cried, and the cat did not understand why she was leaving.

I told Ruth's story in the column. "It is a traumatic enough experience for someone to give up a free and independent life in one's own home," I said, "but when such a move entails giving up a furry, feathery, or finny friend of many years, it is cruel."

I thought about Bethany's no-pet policy. Authorities on aging all over the country have been pointing out for some time that pets in retirement and nursing homes contribute to the well-being of the residents, yet Bethany wouldn't even allow a canary. I mentioned how I had put my name on the waiting list years before and how annually I receive a letter wanting to know when I am coming. "'Not until Edith can come,' I tell them once a year," I said.

Representative Davis was floored by all the opposition to his bill and withdrew it before the column could get into the paper, but who am I to waste a good column? I ran it anyhow.

The column appeared one Saturday morning. On Monday this letter arrived:

Dear Mrs. Young,

I live in a senior citizen's complex (I'm eighty) where we are allowed to have cats. The rules state that we must deposit three hundred dollars, and the cat must be declawed and spayed or neutered.

My children helped me with the deposit, and I finished paying it in monthly installments. My daughter and I went to SICSA and adopted a big Maine Coon cat. He is the only four-footed resident in the building and gets lots of attention. I can't begin to tell you the joy and companionship he has brought into my life. I am not a person who rails at circumstances that left me a widow many years ago, and when I have to make a change in my life style, I never look back. There is, however, bound to be a lonely hour here and there no matter how 'up' one tries to be. Rascal takes care of those hours. He is not a lap cat, and one pets him only when he says it is all right. Nevertheless he is loyal and loving. He has a gourmet's appetite, so his food costs nearly as much as mine, but I don't begrudge him one bite.

At the moment he has given up trying to coax me into the bedroom so he can help me make the bed and is lying on his back with his big furry feet planted firmly on the back of my recliner chair. I would like to train him to harness and take him out for walks, but he says a definite no to such an idea.

Sincerely,

Rose Byrkett

I thought about Rose and Rascal, snug in their apartment, and remembered the dear little wheelchair lady at Bethany who had tears in her eyes when she said to me, "I had a cat before I came here."

The telephone rang. "This is Hannelore Siebert," a bright voice said. "I called to tell you that Edith will be welcome at Bethany in one of the cottages or in the new Homestead apartments."

The walls of Jericho had crumbled. "My goodness," was all I could say.

"Of course we read your column," she went on, "and we all had a good laugh at your timing. The trustees had voted last Wednesday, but no announcement had been made. If you want to come out and look around at any time, please do."

Two days later I received a brochure announcing the opening of a new apartment building at Bethany. The photographs and floor plans looked so inviting that I drove out to take a look.

An apartment with a patio on the ground floor, with a little garden area and right on a lake with a fountain and ducks swimming around was available.

I happened to have enough in my checking account to make a payment to reserve the apartment for Edith and me, and I wrote a check.

Then I hurried home to break the news. I gave Edith three treats and then three more to celebrate. I hugged her and kissed her and told her all about the new apartment and the ducks on the lake. "You never saw a lake or a duck," I told her. "Imagine that."

"Eow," said Edith.

Appendix

This is Edith's favorite Christmas story. Every year on Christmas Eve, with a fire popping and crackling in the fireplace, the colored lights glowing and Edith happy digesting her Christmas meal of oyster bisque, I read it to her.

The Best Bed
Sylvia Townsend Warner

The cat had known many winters, but none like this. Through two slow darkening months it had rained, and now, on the eve of Christmas, the wind had gone round to the east and instead of rain, sleet and hail fell.

The hard pellets hit his drenched sides and bruised them. He ran faster. When boys threw stones at him he could escape by running; but from this heavenly lapidation there was no escape. He was hungry, for he had had no food since he had happened upon a dead sparrow, dead of cold, three days ago. It had not been the cat's habit to eat dead meat, but having fallen upon evil days he had been thankful even for that unhealthy-tasting flesh. Thirst tormented him, worse than hunger. Every now and then he would stop and scrape the frozen gutter with his tongue. He had given up all hope now, he had forgotten all his wiles. He despaired, and ran on.

The lights, the footsteps on the pavement, the crashing buses, the swift cars like the monster cats whose eyes could outstare him, daunted him. Though a Londoner, he was not used to these things, for he was born by the Thames' side and had spent his days among the docks, a modest, useful life of rat-catching and secure slumbers upon flour sacks. But one night the wharf where he lived had caught fire; and terrified by flames, smoke, and uproar, he had begun to run, till by morning he was far from the river and homeless, and too unversed in the ways of the world to find himself another home.

A street door opened, and he flinched aside, and turned a corner. But in that street, doors were opening, too, every door letting out a horror. For it was closing time. Once, earlier in his wanderings, he had crouched by such a door, thinking that any shelter would be better than the rainy street. Before he had time to escape, a hand snatched him up and a voice shouted above his head. "Gorblime if the cat hasn't come in for a drink," the voice said. And the cat felt his nostrils thrust into a puddle of something fiery and stinking, that burned in his nostrils and eyes for hours afterward.

He flattened himself against the wall, and lay motionless until the last door should have swung open for the last time. Only when someone walked by, bearing that smell with him, did the cat stir. Then his nose quivered with invincible disgust, his large ears pressed back upon his head, and the tip of his tail beat stiffly upon the pavement. A dog, with its faculty of conscious despair, would have abandoned itself, and lain down to await death; but when the streets were quiet once more the cat ran on.

There had been a time when he ran and leaped for the pleasure of the thing, rejoicing in his strength like an athlete. The resources of that lean, sinewy body, disciplined in the hunting days of his youth, had served him well in the first days of his wandering; then, speeding before some barking terrier, he had hugged amidst his terrors a compact and haughty joy, the knowledge that he could surely outstrip the pursuer; but now his strength would only serve to prolong his torment. Though an unaccumulated fatigue smoldered in every nerve, the obdurate limbs carried him on, and would carry him on still, a captive to himself, meekly trotting to the place of his death.

He ran as the wind directed, turning this way and that to avoid the gusts, spiked with hail, that ravened through the streets. His eyes were closed, but suddenly at a familiar sound he stopped and stiffened with fear. It was the sound of a door swinging on its hinges. He sniffed apprehensively. There was a smell, puffed out with every swinging-to of the door, but it was not the smell he abhorred; and though he waited in the shadow of a buttress, no sounds of jangling voices came to confirm his fears, and though the door continued to open and shut, no footsteps came from it. He stepped cautiously from his buttress into a porch. The smell was stronger here. It was aromatic, rich, and a little smoky. It tickled his nose and made him sneeze.

The door was swinging with the wind. The aperture was small, too small for anything to be seen through it, save only a darkness that was not quite dark. With a sudden determination the cat flitted through.

Of his first sensations, one overpowered all the others. Warmth! It poured over him, it penetrated his being, and confused his angular physical consciousness of cold and hunger and fatigue into something rounded and indistinct. Flooded with weariness, he sank down on the stone flags.

Another sneezing-fit roused him. He jumped up, and began to explore.

The building he was in reminded him of home. Often, hunting the riverside, he had strayed into places like this — lofty and dusky, stonefloored and securely uninhabited. But they had smelled of corn, of linseed, of tallow, of sugar; none of them smelt as this did, smokily sweet. They had been cold. Here it was warm. They had been dark; and here the dusk was mellowed with one red star, burning in midair, and with the glimmer of a few tapers that added to the smoky sweetness their smell of warm wax.

His curiosity growing with his confidence, the cat ran eagerly about the church. He rubbed his back against the font, he examined the varying smell of the hassocks, he trotted up the pulpit stairs, sprang on the ledge, and sharpened his claws in the cushion. Outside the wind boomed, and the hail clattered against the windows, but within the air was warm and still, and the red star burned mildly on. Over against the pulpit the cat came on something that reminded him even more of home — a wisp of hay, lying on the flags. He had often seen hay; sometimes borne towering above the greasy tide on barges; sometimes fallen from the nosebags of the great draught horses who waited so peacefully in the wharfingers' yards.

The hay seemed to have fallen from a box on trestles, cut out of unstained wood. The cat stood on his hind

legs, and tried to look in, but it was too high for him.
He turned about, but his curiosity brought him back
again, and poising himself on his clustered paws, he
rocked slightly, gauging his spring, and then jumped,
alighting softly upon a bed of hay. He landed so
delicately that though the two kneeling figures at either
end of the crib swayed forward, they did not topple over.
The cat sniffed them, a trifle suspiciously, but they did
not hold his attention long. It was the hay that interested
him. A drowsy scent rose out of the deep, warm bed as
he kneaded and shuffled it with his forepaws. This, this,
promised him what he had so long yearned for; sound
sleep, an enfolding in warmth and softness, a nourishing
forgetfulness. He paced round in a small circle, burrow-
ing himself a close nest, purring with a harsh note of
joy. As he turned he brushed against a third figure in
the crib; but he scarcely noticed it. Already a rapture of
sleepiness was overcoming him; the two kneeling figures
had done him no harm, nor would this reposing one.
Soon the bed was made to his measure. Bowing his head
upon his paws, he abandoned himself.

Another onslaught of hail dashed against the
windows, the door creaked, and at a gust of wind
entering the church, the candle flames wavered as
though they were nodding their heads in assent; but
though the cat's ears flicked once or twice against the

feet of the plaster Jesus, he was too securely asleep to know or heed.

I tell Edith that I like to think the next morning when the sexton came to make the church ready for Christmas services, he gave the cat a bowl of warm cream and the priest appointed him church mouse-catcher for the rest of his life.

Bibliography

Baker, Hettie Gray. *195 Cat Tales*, New York: Farrar, Straus and Young, 1953

Bartlett, John. *Familiar Quotations, Fourteenth Edition*, Boston, Toronto: Little, Brown, and Co., 1968

Chandoha, Walter. *The Literary Cat*, Philadelphia: Lippincott, 1977

Camuti, Louis J. *Park Avenue Vet*, New York: Holt, Rinehart and Winston, 1967

Clarke, Frances Elizabeth. *Cats — and Cats: Great Cat Stories of Our Day*, New York: The Macmillan Co., 1937

Davis, Elmer. *Not to Mention the War*, Indianapolis, New York: The Bobbs-Merrill Co., 1940

Eliot, T. S. *Old Possum's Book of Practical Cats*, New York: Harcourt, Brace, and Jovanovich, 1982

Ellman, Richard, editor. *The New Oxford Book of American Verse*, New York: Oxford University Press, 1976

Fleischer, Leonore. *The Cat's Pajamas*, New York: Harper & Row, 1982

Foster, Dorothy, comp. *In Praise of Cats*, New York: Crown Publishers, Inc. 1974

Frazier, Anitra, with Norma Eckrote. *The Natural Cat: A Holistic Guide for Finicky Owners*, San Francisco: Harbor Publishing Co., 1981

Gallico, Paul. *Jennie*, New York: Penquin Books, 1930

Gooden, Mona, comp. *The Poet's Cat*, Freeport, N.Y.: Books for Libraries Press, 1969

Kalstone, Shirlee. *Cats: Breeds, Care and Behavior*, New York: Dell Publishing Co., 1983

Lockridge, Frances and Richard. *Cats and People*, Philadelphia: J. B. Lippincott Co., 1950

Morris, Desmond. *Catlore*, New York: Crown Publishers, Inc., 1987

Newman, Larry. "Feline Fame Aside, Where's Edith?"; "Happy 1986! It's the Cat's Meow." Dayton, Ohio: *The Journal Herald*, December 29, 1985; January 1, 1986

Noyes, Alfred. *Collected Poems*, Philadelphia: J. B. Lippencott Co., 1947

Pond, Grace and Angela Sayer. *The Intelligent Cat*, New York: The Dial Press, 1977

Sarton, May. *The Fur Person*, Boston: G. K. Bell, 1988

Swinburne, Algernon Charles. *Poems and Ballads*, London: Chatto & Windus, 1907

Untermeyer, Louis. *Modern American Poetry*, New York: Harcourt, Brace and Co., 1925

Van Vechten, Carl. *Tiger in the House*, New York: A. A. Knopf, 1920

Warner, Charles Dudley. *My Summer in a Garden*, Boston and New York: Houghton, Mifflin and Co., 1890

Warner, Sylvia Townsend. *Letters*, New York: Viking Press, 1982

_____. *The Salutation*. New York: Viking Press, 1932.

Wells, Carolyn and Louella D. Everett. *The Cat in Verse*, Boston: Little, Brown and Co., 1935

Withycomb, E. G. *The Oxford Dictionary of English Christian Names*, Oxford: The Clarendon Press, 1977

Yeats, William Butler. *Collected Poems*, New York: The Macmillan Co., 1919

Rosamond Young was born in Dayton, the daughter of Harry and Isabel McPherson. Her father was a commercial artist and her mother was a writer and teacher. Ms. Young graduated from Steele High School and Oberlin College, and taught English, Latin, German, and journalism, mostly at Stivers High School in Dayton. She resigned after thirty years to become a columnist for *The Journal Herald*, and retired as staff columnist of *The Dayton Daily News* in 1982 where she continues to write a weekly column. She is the author of twelve books, including two series of English textbooks and four biographies. She enjoys the splendid dualities of gardening and traveling.